"I had the privilege of teaching through Revelation in a restricted country. Teaching through the book to pastors who would almost certainly end up in prison (or worse) brought the book to life. Susan's poems don't flinch from the doubt and despair of this life but redirect our gaze to the cross of Christ that won our freedom. I hope you will be as encouraged by this collection as I have been."

—**Rob Novak**, Senior Pastor, Resurrection Presbyterian Church, San Diego

"I came to Susan's work looking for what her poems could add to my appreciation of the book of Revelation. I was not disappointed. I now think regular poetry would be a wonderful supplement to any reading of Revelation. Poetry like this brings home the themes of the book and adds a needed depth of feeling. Susan's creative, startling, delightful images fascinate long enough for her message to get through our natural defense of avoiding honest pain. Some selections, like 'Unmasked,' are examples of the fine art that can rise out of shared suffering. The work is decidedly positive, as the themes of the gospel are never far away, finding God's chosen response intertwined in every human need."

—**Glenn Parkinson**, Pastor Emeritus, Severna Park Presbyterian Church (PCA), and author of *Tapestry: The Book of Revelation* and *A Larger Faith: The Book of Daniel*

"Susan Erikson's best book of poetry thus far! I particularly like the poems 'The Digger' and 'The Holy War.' Every pastor or teacher of the Bible ought to have a copy of this insightful book!"

—**S. Louise Chestnut**, Section Violist, Annapolis Symphony Orchestra, and instrumental accompanist, Safe Harbor Presbyterian Church

"The author creatively expresses the practical message of Revelation, a book that offers us needed hope during troubled times. These poems are word pictures of truth that express powerful human emotions. We especially enjoyed 'Sardis,' 'The Stumbling Church,' and 'Unmasked.'"

—**James R. Newheiser**, Associate Professor of Christian Counseling and Pastoral Theology, Reformed Theological Seminary, Charlotte, North Carolina and Caroline Newheiser, Christian Counselor, Biblical Counseling Coalition

"I read Susan Erikson's book three times. The author uses the effectiveness of poetry to untangle current chaos in such scope and depth. It is so timely for me."

—**Faming Xu**, friend and prayer partner

"*Reflections on Revelation* reminds us that our sin poses a greater danger than any virus. No matter how many precautions we take, all of them pale in comparison to our need for salvation and the promises that God makes to all who trust in Christ. May this collection of poems encourage and strengthen your faith."

—**Noah Michael Fate-Cloud**, Bible college graduate and seminary student, Knox Theological Seminary

Reflections on Revelation in the Time of COVID

Reflections on Revelation in the Time of COVID

Finding Hope When Life Is Hard

Susan E. Erikson

RESOURCE *Publications* • Eugene, Oregon

REFLECTIONS ON REVELATION IN THE TIME OF COVID
Finding Hope When Life Is Hard

Resource Publications
An Imprint of Wipf and Stock Publishers
199 W. 8th Ave., Suite 3
Eugene, OR 97401

www.wipfandstock.com

PAPERBACK ISBN: 978-1-6667-0213-2
HARDCOVER ISBN: 978-1-6667-0214-9
EBOOK ISBN: 978-1-6667-0215-6

05/24/21

Dedication

If 2020 taught us anything, it was that life can be an overwhelming experience. I doubt if 2021 will be any different. We need a hope that transcends all our struggles in this life, and we have it in God's extravagant gifts. First and of primary importance, He gave us His Son and the redeeming work of the Cross. Then, He gave us each other. You are a gift to me. I am a gift to you. We are the Church, the living, breathing, body of Christ, and it is a marvelous grace of God.

Some of us teach. Others encourage. Some are great listeners and offer much needed wisdom. Some have the amazing ability to call us out when we goof up, and we are willing to listen. Some fix meals, clean toilets, ferry those in need to doctor appointments. Some are dedicated to prayer. And many just live their difficult lives transparently in front us. They let us see their pain, their frustration, their moments of fear and discouragement, and their ultimate endurance. I have been the beneficiary over the years of so many of these wonderfully gifted people and continue to be constantly grateful that God allows me to love and encourage others as my walk intersects with theirs.

This book is dedicated to the Church, God's glorious family. As God is transforming us through the working of the Holy Spirit, He is turning our shared suffering into endurance, our endurance into character, and our impatient, struggling character, into His powerful hope that will carry us through. And we can confidently draw near to God's throne, knowing that He will provide the mercy and grace we need in time of need. Together we will make it securely home.

Contents

Acknowledgments

First, I want to thank my husband, Larry, for being a great copyeditor and listening ear. I am always asking him to listen to me read my paragraphs aloud as I slog toward "the best copy." I am forever grateful for his love and encouragement.

Secondly, I want to thank my mother, Sylvia Elder, and my son, Raymond Erikson, for their general editing. They come to editing from completely different perspectives, which consistently brings out my best work. I am so blessed to have you both.

Thirdly, I want to thank Marilyn Segraves for being the kind of friend who always inspires my best writing. She got me started on this book and has been a wonderful sounding board all the way through.

Introduction

I am penning these poems in the middle of a global pandemic. We have not only been experiencing widespread quarantines and economic disruptions, but large—scale protests, riots, and violence. Lawlessness and fear are the air we breathe, and many are calling evil good, and good, evil. (Isa 5:20) The book of Revelation is on our minds, and believers wonder if we are on the cusp of the Second Coming. Of course, Christians have been wondering this since the early church! We are not the first generation to suffer persecution, disease, and the general unsettledness that comes with living in a sinful world that crackles with spiritual warfare. We may not be the last.

Revelation is a good book for hard times because it was written to encourage those living through those times. It offers one clear answer—Christ, the one who is, who was, and is to come. He is the firstborn from the dead, and the ruler over all kings on earth. He is the beginning of all history and the one who will bring it all to an end. Christ rules over the church. He is the only one able to open the scroll and reveal to His people what God has kept secret. He is both the Lion of Judah, the fulfillment of the royal house of David, and the Lamb, the one whose sacrifice brings His people into His kingdom. Christ is the one who will bring war and judgment against all wickedness, and a new heaven and new earth for those who belong to Him. Revelation calls us to bring our sorrows, our struggles, our fears, our victories, our failures, our praise, all of it before our Savior, and lay them at His feet.

Revelation is not so much about matching current events to verses, but about fully living in Christ, bringing His grace and truth into our life's most difficult circumstances. On Christ's last night He told his disciples, and by extension the church, to expect hardship and suffering, but that He had already overcome the world. Christ's perfect obedience, His sacrifice on the Cross, His resurrection and ascension, conquered Satan down to the enemy's rebellious core and gave our accuser a mortal blow. The Lamb's sacrifice in blood forever covers us, secures our eternal redemption, provides the armor necessary to conquer day to day living, and guarantees our ultimate freedom from the destructive effects of sin.

It should also protect our hearts from fear, because in Revelation we see our frightening world under God's control. Revelation tells us that our war with evil may look huge and overwhelming, but to God it is only a mopping—up operation. The victory was decided long ago at the Cross, and God has already won. We are not in the battle alone. Ever. "He who is in you is greater than he who is in the world." (1 Jn 4:4) All the evil principalities and powers can do is harry the church and make war on her until Satan will be decisively defeated and thrown into the lake of fire at the end of all things. We need to hear that assurance when we are in the trenches. It gives us strength to keep fighting, and a great hope that "presses on toward the goal for the prize of the upward call of God in Christ Jesus." (Phil 3:14)

Revelation gives us the truest, most delightful happy ending that could have ever been imagined. In the end it is not about the seven seals or seven bowls, but our eternal dwelling place with God. "He will dwell with them, and they will be his people, and God himself will be with them as their God. He will wipe away every tear from their eyes, and death shall be no more, neither shall there be mourning, nor crying, nor pain anymore, for the former things have passed away." (Rev 21:3-4) It is a glorious picture of real hope in the face of challenging trial.

As you read, notice that each poem includes references to not only the chapter of Revelation that is being addressed, but to other Scriptures that connect to that poem, to our life in Christ, and to our trials. Consider the references an invitation to explore the Word of God when you need help most. Look up the passages, discover how Scripture unpacks itself, and find comfort as God speaks His grace to you.

I Need You LORD

I will rejoice and be glad in your steadfast love, because you have seen my affliction; you have known the distress of my soul, and you have not delivered me into the hand of the enemy; you have set my feet in a broad place.

—Ps 31:7–8

The Spirit of the Age[1]

I feel as if the world is falling down a rabbit hole,
And I am Alice,
Tumbling right behind.

Are You there, LORD?
My soul is full of troubles.

I understand this world is not a gentle place.
For sin has roughed the edges raw,
Has sanded down the quiet hills,
Has bent the trees,
Unearthed the mountains
underneath the tugging,
Wrestling pressures of the Curse,
And left us jagged boundaries,
Sharp and restless borders,
Pushing,
Pulling,
Cataclysmic wills demanding,
Re—defining what was right
becoming What is Mine,

1. Ps 88

Until all human thoughts and deeds
express an awkward shape,
A monstrous wonderland design.

I need you, LORD.

This wayward turning world seems vicious,
More intensely underlined,
More rough,
More angry,
Recently more violent.
I have felt the earnestness of darkness
spreading more and more,
Surrounding intellect and heart,
Its tangling,
Clinging pull,
Confounding noble thought,
Its brash and bragging overriding simple truth
where even People of the Book
are falling through,
Are crumpling down,
Are floundering,
Hesitant and locked in fear.

And I contend
(if only silent conversations in my head)
with this world's minor prophets,
Seers of the news and social media,

Panderers of broken wisdom

crying in the streets,

Demanding that we eat

their doomed philosophies as royal feasts.

Is this the end?

Is this the time You will appear?

The Digger[1]

He is digging again.
Marking out the trench,
Uncovering all the rubble underneath.

It all looks calm and peaceful up above,
A grassy field,
A wide and ever—expanding lawn of green,
In rolling hills and valleys,
Undulating pasture
capturing a summer breeze,
Dancing to a music only swaying trees can hear.

Eden above.

But scrape away the soil,
Excavate the layers deeply laid
beneath such grass,
Reveals the death below.
The broken, scattered pottery,
The coins,
The piece of glass,
The piles of stones.
(It used to be a wall.)

1. Hab 1:5

This part was pavement.
See those terra cotta tiles,
A roof collapsed so long ago.

And then the bones.
The proof of our mortality
is jutting through the dirt,
And men and women speculate
about the story underground.
What happened here?
The clues abound
as bits and broken pieces of a life
describe a long—forgotten world,
Their shadows tracing yesterday.

What have we found?

We found ourselves.
We are the dig.
We are the tumbled rubble underneath,
The broken clues
to our own lost humanity.
The grasses up above us lie,
As layer upon layer cover up,
Obliterate the stench beneath,
The awful smell,
The Tel that chronicles our striving,
Building,
Climbing from the endless trench,

I NEED YOU LORD—*THE DIGGER*

The mound details our need to hide,
Burying ourselves in ever—glorious strata,
Cold,
Unending cold,
Lost and defective souls our dig bequeaths.

We need the dig.
We need the Digger.
Carving out,
Revealing,
Sifting out the twists and turns that mark our lives.
We want to only see the lawn,
The garden fantasy on which our empty ego thrives.
But first,
The rubble must be tamed,
The dirt removed,
The broken pottery described.
We must be found the way we truly are.
For only then the dig redeems.

The Digger, lovingly,
Unpacks,
Explains,
Reclaims.
For only He can move the stones,
Rebuild the flesh,
And gather dust to dust beneath the earth
to rise to blood and bones.
Only He drags shame from dirt.

Only He can seize and crush our seething hurt and shake it off.

Only He restores our artifacts of soul to breath.

And death,

Undone,

No longer hides beneath.

We are above,

At last an Eden truly real.

Someday the digging will completely cease.

Someday the meadow grasses

will all bend and sway to melodies

the Digger sings

before a waking earth,

As opened trenches now release

their bodies,

Those who have been waiting for His call and their rebirth.

No bones.

No stones.

No broken pots.

No dust.

No dirt.

No buried hurt.

But dancers, glorious dancers crowding heath,

Their ears, their mouths, and feet in sweet delight

before the Digger's love and cosmic mirth.

Sharper Than Any Two—Edged Sword[1]

Gleaning again,
Through an extravagant harvest,
A harvest of sacred books.
Letting His words
all dance and skip across my mind.
Letting them sink,
And settling,
Secure good roots within my heart,
A vibrant cinema of stories,
Writing and re—writing how I see,
How to clearly contemplate and understand
all that is mystery.
Playing,
Teaching,
Transporting me to unknown places,
Giving me
a new perspective
on the times and spaces I was sure I knew,
But only kissed the freeway,
Skated past,
And did not really notice
just what kind of universe,
What kind of roads

1. Pss 1:1–2; 19:7–11; 119:25–32; Heb 4:12

were there for following,

Were waiting to be found,

Be carefully consumed,

Be chewed so thoughtfully to make their flavors last,

So I could walk

just where He wanted me to be.

Kyrie Eleison[1]

I love to open up Your Word.
It feels like
opening the back door on a summer day,
The air perfumed
by all the fragrances of grace
that rise up from each passing bloom,
The many songs of birds in praise,
The fluttering leaves,
And bending grass.
I am awake,
Aware,
That God,
That You alone
are waiting near,
To catch my eye,
To take my hand,
And laughing,
Take me running in the fields,
Climbing higher,
Every new adventure leading closer
to the supper of the Lamb,
To where the Bride comes,
Finally,

1. Ps 51:1–4, 12

To wed the Groom.

I love to open up Your Word.
But as I come so close to You,
I see my sin,
And I am crushed.
I thought I'd done these marvelous things
for You.

They were for me.

I thought enthusiasm
to explain Your glorious truths,
Your mercy,
Steadfast love,
To teach and share Your story,
Opening doors to letting summer sun
shine in on others on this struggling walk,
Was all for You.
But I was also there,
Intruding,
Standing in the way of grace.
Notice me,
My heart was saying.
Notice me,
Not Him.
How interesting,
How terrible of me
to point to You,

To praise the Son,
But cast my shadow on the room.
I am undone.

I love to open up Your Word.
I know Your summer sun
is leaning on my door.
I need Your help.
Have mercy on me, Lord.
You led me to myself.
I see I am iniquity,
Too often brilliant on the outside,
Restlessly self—centered underneath.
Against You only,
I have sinned.
Lord, set me free.
I know,
In mercy You have covered me with sacrificial blood,
Your blood.
Forgive my heart,
(the idol in this place).
Forgive,
Remind me of Your great salvation,
Give me joy.
Renew Your new creation once again,
And scrub away all lingering aroma
of the tomb.

I love to open up Your Word.

And Moses Said[1]

And Moses says,
I tremble through and through with fear
before His blazing fire,
Thunder,
Tempest,
Roaring out His power,
Terrifying holiness too near,
Too close,
His presence
easily devours soul and flesh.
His flaming entourage,
The Heavenly Host,
Surrounds His throne.
I cannot see His face and live.
The mountain should have buried me.
Instead,
Somehow,
I am completely covered,
Sheltered in the rocky cleft,
While Love Divine is passing by.

1. Rev 1; Exod 3:1–6, 19:9–25, 33:18–23; Isa 6:1–7; Col 1:13–14; Heb 12:18–21; 1 John 1: 1–4

And I,
Like lost Isaiah,
Cry,
Oh, woe is me!
Unclean! Unclean!
I need Your grace.
I need Your mercy every moment,
Every hour.
Have mercy on me, Holy One!
Have mercy, God, on me.

Christ is the hand that shielded
me from death,
Who let the fire fall on Him,
And took its scorching burn,
God's holy cup of wrath poured out.
He rescued me.
He satisfied the debt,
And traded sacrifice for grace,
Divorcing certainty from doubt.
Removing shame and guilt,
Cremating,
Turning hell to ash.

And now we see,
Says John,
So close to us we see His face.
We are not harmed.
We touched Him with our hands.

15

We heard Him speak.

He says,

See Me.

In truth, you see the Father.

What rash,

Yet reverent boast is this?

How can such cosmic fire

claim a bush that never burns?

How can One bloody sacrifice

undo a rotting tomb of worms?

How can life's mourning,

Crushing suffering,

Rise,

Be raised in power?

Or hearing Holy Speech

release the storm,

And calm the tempest overwhelming me?

Unless He is the Son.

I need Your grace,

Your mercy,

Every moment,

Every hour.

Have mercy on me, Jesus.

I NEED YOU LORD—*AND MOSES SAID*

Alpha and Omega,

He who is,

Who was,

And is to come,

Have mercy, God, on me.

The Church in Christ

But now in Christ Jesus you who once were far off have
been brought near by the blood of Christ . . . And he
came and preached peace to you who were far off and
peace to those who were near. For through him we both
have access in one Spirit to the Father. So then you
are no longer strangers and aliens, but you are fellow
citizens with the saints and members of the household
of God, built on the foundation of the apostles and
prophets, Christ Jesus himself being the cornerstone, in
whom the whole structure, being joined together, grows
into a holy temple in the Lord.

—Eph 2:13, 17–21

Ephesus[1]

Your Word, O Lord,
Is truth,
And we would guard it
like Bereans,
Eagerly examining the Scriptures,
Daily studying
to rightly handle every line
that You designed to light our path.
We know it well.

Be careful in unpacking
what the testimonies say.
Test them,
Be discerning,
Ever learning,
Do not stray beyond the fence,
Wall all things in with dutiful propriety,
Let holiness define the righteous road.

The Son of Man
is come in brilliant light.
The Word of God is living,
Active,

1 Heb 4:12; Rev 2:1–7

Sharper than two—edged swords,

Piercing all,

Discerning thoughts,

His eyes,

Like flaming fire,

Sees.

He knows.

I know your works,

Your toil.

I know you patiently endure,

And bear all things for my name's sake.

Alas,

The sin infects the sinner saved.

Your vigilance in doctrine

and endurance,

Cannot keep your pride at bay,

And easily defiles those gracious parts.

There is no barter here but my own blood

to render grace.

My holiness cannot be sold.

You have no love.

You have forgotten piety and zeal

without my grace is cold.

Smyrna[1]

Every day our brothers and our sisters die,
Are slaughtered in the streets,
Their plight ignored by nations
more concerned by daily comforts
and their dull deceits.
We are exposed.
It's over there. It is not here.

The churches shuttered down,
Some leveled to the ground
in some worlds,
Powerful officials claiming
crimes against the state.
All religions now must carefully align,
Agree to party lines
and sign their loyalty away.
Whom do you serve?
Allegiance stretches faith and raises fear.

The Word of God
reminds that in this world
the face of persecution sometimes wears a sword.
And martyrdom may be

1. Rev 2:8–11

the path that leads to your reward.

Stay faithful, true.
Dear Christian, trust your Savior.
This, the acrid taste of Jesus' love
still bites.
It tests.
Its work refines.
Your sweet endurance
is a gracious thing before the Father's sight.
His thoughts toward you
are words of grace.
No evil stands
that He has not already claimed,
Restrained,
Is not intended to destroy,
But to establish you in Him,
To stand like steel and wear His name,
To shine with peace
before a frightened world.
You are His overcomers.
Death may reach its mighty arm,
But nothing separates His love from you.
Face your strife.
He will enable each
to bear this pain.
The first death cannot touch the soul,
Or any in this world control,
For you have gained the crown of life.

Pergamum[1]

There is a grand romance,
A sacred,
Cosmic Love
initiated by our God
toward us.
He is the one who courts,
We are the one pursued.
We are the ones that Jesus loves.

Yet we too often
are the ones
too easily beguiled by siren songs
that lure our wandering hearts
to lovers of convenience,
Paramours in dangerous games.

How can you bow
before your sexual immorality,
And claim to bear His holy name?
Why do you seek your freedom
by consuming sacrifices meant for lesser gods?
Do you not have a watchful eye
on weaker ones among the flock

1. Heb 4:12; Rev 2:12–17

that Jesus loves?
You all profess disdain
for wicked teaching,
Yet you let its treacheries
seduce and shape your freedoms,
In defiance of your Holy Lover's
rightful claims.
Why give your heart a place
for spiritual adultery,
And turn your worship into shame?

The Son of Man is
come in brilliant light.
He sees.
He knows.
I will make cruel war
against the Nicolatians,
Against deceivers and defilers
rising from the fires of Satan's throne.
I am already walking in your midst.
I am already intervening,
Purifying judgments
dripping on the edge of eager blades.
Repent.
Believe, and worship Me.
To you, beloved,
To those confounded by such
small,
And cheaply gained pretensions,

Do not covet lesser things
that rend our tender fellowship,
And turn my Manna into stone.
Fascination with this barren, hungry world—
It surely dies.
I AM temptation's adversary,
Champion in Word and Deed,
The sword that surely separates
the lie from life,
And soul from death.
I AM the one who gives you breath.
Behold,
I AM the One Who Conquers,
I alone
the One that Feeds and Satisfies.

Thyatira[1]

The harvest is plentiful,
But workers
are few.
Pray to the Lord,
The Lord of the Harvest
to send His laborers
into the fields,
To preach good news,
To love and engage.

Lord of the Harvest,
Let us be hands,
Let us be feet.
We love the weary,
The hungry,
The many whose hearts
are longing for grace.
Alert to injustice,
We share our abundance to gather all in,
We call out redemption from sorrow and sin.

I know of your works,
Your love

1. Matt 9:35–38; Rev 2:18–29

and your service,
Your patient endurance wherever God leads.
You love broken people,
You notice their stumbling.
Embracing their sorrows,
You capture the gospel in merciful deeds.

I have this against you.
Your heresy wounds
and the words defame.
She who has stomach for worldly indulgence,
Who drinks concupiscence,
And eats at tables where idols play,
And truth is shamed,
You have not displaced her,
Or reined her in.
She will not yield.
Thus, the rankest weeds
between good seeds,
Are crowding your harvest out of the field.
She will not repent,
So, on her head I heap great ill.
Her spiritual offspring,
Those who desire Satan's offering,
They will be cut and thrown on the pyre.

The Son of Man
has eyes of fire,
Flames that search both heart and mind.

He sees.

He knows.

He will not keep this worthless chaff,

But cast it out,

Let the flames fly up,

As the tempest blows.

But to the wheat:

My precious harvest—

Hold fast to Me

until I come.

To those who conquer

through My Spirit,

Keep My Words until the end.

You who preach with hands and feet,

You are protected from My war.

I give to you,

With Me,

The right to rule the mighty nations.

I give Myself.

To you I AM your Morning Star.

Sardis[1]

Around the Corner

It used to be the Methodist church
on the corner.
A thriving place,
A warm community of grace
where neighbors met each week
to praise the Lord,
To hear the Word
and worship at the feet of Christ.

Now it is a modest office selling real estate.
It might as well be
one of this street's many stores.
The shape,
The brick of this old building
echoes back to other days.
Without the cross it seems forlorn.
The stained—glass windows still remain.
Their presence stain,
Somehow rebuke its present phase.
Some sell old houses.
Where is the rescue station welcoming the lost

1. Rev 3:1–6

for Jesus' sake?
Driving by,
I almost do a double—take.
Is this a church?

Down the Street

Born as meetinghouses,
Rural congregations
built their basic buildings,
Simple wooden structures
painted white,
With one straight spire
pointing lives toward heaven,
Lifting eyes to Christ.
Often isolated,
Parishes surviving in the wilderness,
They understood their pilgrim state.
Gathering each week,
(Some by horse,
But many coming eagerly by feet),
They came with thankful hearts.
They came to sing,
They came to pray,
They came to eat and drink the grace of God,
To feel the aches and pains of daily sin
be covered by His blood.

THE CHURCH IN CHRIST—*SARDIS*

One generation lifted up,

One generation lost in place,

Already wandering away.

From year to year,

From son to son,

The little church sustained,

And lost.

Sustained,

And lost.

Now very few new people come.

The steady twenty—five

has dwindled down to eight,

And they aren't sure

just why they congregate.

And one might wonder

if the blessed and sanctified

are waiting in their graves

(beside the edifice,

Across the lawn,

Well—situated under leaning stones,

Protected by the decorated iron fence)

for heaven's resurrection day,

Or only sleeping

as they slept each Sabbath,

Unaware a reckoning is waiting at the gate.

The building leans to match the graves.

Is this a church?

In Town

Two hundred years of laying stone,
Of building,
Carving intricate designs,
The flying buttresses
all lifting vaulted ceiling to the skies.
The many spires raise our eyes,
And stained—glass windows illustrate the gospel,
Story after story,
Word in picture,
Reaching people's lives.

There also are distractions,
Elaborate graves within the nave,
Memorials and crypts
commemorate the notables and knowns,
The patron kings,
Important people's bones.
It seems a better monument to man
than messages of grace,
A vast museum
sharing memories of kings instead of Christ.
Religion serving artifacts like tasty tidbits,
Potluck,
All the interesting tastes and views
that might be gospel life.

It looks so grandly churchy
in its sturdiness.
A standing stone
to Jesus' own,
From age to age the same.
Surely many souls
who worshipped here
are truly His.
They walk with Him in victory,
Their names securely written in the Book of Life,
Eternally, the truest church,
Forever will remain.

But one might wonder,
Listening to angelic choirs,
Reading Jesus' precious words
while tourists wandering in
and out,
Examine remnants of forgotten creed
(those rites that blessed
each coronation,
Every grand procession,
Ritually dispensed
on Sunday after Sunday),
Left too many blind,
Too many deaf.
Too many colder than the stones,
The standing stones that wrapped their hearts and flesh.

That grand invention blotting out
the simple truth:
The blood and sacrifice of Christ,
His glorious resurrection
raising us,
Destroying death.

Exhibits in an old museum,
They cannot hear,
They cannot see,
So many lost,
And few who understand are left.
Is this a church?

Philadelphia[1]

The government would seek
to mute our praising tongues.
They would restrain
even our hearts from prayer.
Our pastors
labor in the camps,
In prisons.

Keep them steadfast,
Keep Your people from despair.

Now death has set its roving eyes on us.
It stalks the streets.
No masks,
No washing hands
can keep its seething mouth from stealing breath.
It takes!
It takes!
Even our old oppressors
shake before its crushing jaws.
We are alone.
We throw our weary souls on You.
We won't renounce Your name,

1. Rev 3:7–13

We love Your Word.
We are so weak,
Our faith is raw,
We barely stand on aching feet.
Can this old, anguished world reach up to heaven's throne?

Those who shuttered daily prayer,
Who tried to regulate
your worship here,
Or claim your heart—
These men will come to you for help.
(This is your opportunity to speak.
Your mouths are free because of Me,
In life or death.)
These men will know that
I have loved you from the start,
And loved you more.
Before you stands an open door
that reaches to eternity.
No one can shut what I unbar.
I have the key.
I have complete authority.
You wear my name,
You are my own.
Hold fast!
Hold fast!
Hold fast to Me!
You are the conquerors,
Unwavering,
Not even death can take you from My holy grasp.

Laodicea[1]

Behold,
The bountiful and colorful displays
of fruits and vegetables,
Where every day is Market Day,
And never emptying shelves
all overflow with
oranges, potatoes, onions, celery,
Assorted greens
(in bags or loosely placed for someone finicky)!
How about the cereal aisle?
Which grain to buy?
House brand or ad appeal?
More natural?
More sugary?
No GMO, or additives,
Some gluten free,
An overwhelming panoply
of stuff
to bag and carry home.

See how much we have!
A self—sufficient people,
Prospering so well that

1. Isa 55:1; Rev 3:14–22

even poor and ill fare better here
than many citizens of Mother Rome.

We even faced adversity
and conquered it ourselves.
No need for help,
We thank You for Your interest
in our welfare.
We are fine.
Robust economy prepared us,
Made us capable to conquer
any possible contingency.

Except for Mine.

Prosperity has made you blind.
Autonomy has made you weak.
You do not seek My face
to meet your needs,
Depending on
a strength you do not own,
But only wear because
I lovingly bestowed its grace.
You live on mercy,
Not your pharmaceuticals,
Your textiles,
Nor your GDP.
The sum of human capital
is not enough
to meet the longings

thirsty souls are crying for.
I could be standing at your door,
Requesting you to join My feast.
You aren't prepared.
You need me more than
anything this world can make or sell.
Your paper—thin commodities
will decompose to earth
(like you),
Dissolve,
Disintegrate,
Their value sifted and forgotten
like the dust that falls through every digger's sieve.
Before My face,
You are the poor,
The blind,
The naked,
Searching,
Never finding,
Never holding firmly to the riches,
Incomparable,
That only I can give.
Why seek to be complete
with what can never fill or satisfy?

Come everyone who thirsts,
Come to My waters,
Come to Me.
He who has no money,
Come.

Buy wine and milk,
Buy without money,
Without price,
For your delight must be in Me,
Not in your life,
Not in your works,
But Mine.
I freely gift you holy garments.
Wear them.
Let Me cover all your sinfulness and shame.
I AM the healing salve
that lifts the cataracts of guilt from eyes and hearts
so truth and light may enter in.
Only I,
Who love you,
Can release you from
your tendency for self—reliance,
Sovereignty that trades in pain,
And dies in sin.

The Feast is near.
And he who has an ear,
Let him repent!
Let all draw close to hear the Spirit speak.
Be free.
Let go of stuff.
Let nothing bind that keeps you from the Sacred Feast.
Let go of self.
Come near to Me.

Church Awake![1]

Church of Christ,
Wake up!
You have been slumbering
while nations yearned for holy truth,
While people burned.

Like Rip Van Winkle,
Dreaming and forgetting
has surrendered gain,
Has overshadowed sacred calling,
Purpose.
Shattering all your memories of hope.

Without the Word,
Without the proclamation of His grace,
We are indeed cut off.
The market cries for everything but truth.
It cannot save.

We serve the lost.
Behold the dead and dying
gathered at your feet.
Ezekiel's bones,

1. Ezek 37:7–14; 1 Thess 5:1–11

Dried up,

Awaiting promises that only God can keep.

Unknowing that the Lord has come,

Is already at work among the graves.

Unknowing that the sprinkled blood of Christ

is resurrecting,

Transferring Being there,

The Holy Spirit breathing life,

Is conquering despair.

You have been saved,

Redeemed,

Most favored,

Loved beyond all measure.

Wear your underserving treasured status

humbly in the street.

Be known as those who dare to touch the ailing and the dying,

Quick to listen,

Ready to unpack His sacred truth in word,

To give an answer with compassion.

Be His signposts,

Emblems of His faithfulness.

Be wide awake.

Be sober.

Night is coming.

Like a thief, it hunts for prey.

You are not children of the dark,

But of the Day.

The Stumbling Church[1]

We pilgrims
are the things of earth,
The stumbling ones.
So hard to stand in faith,
To be the stable,
Steadfast,
Never shifting from the gospel's hope,
Redeemed elect.

Instead we linger over self,
We savor it,
We see the dark around,
The hate,
The sirens screeching chaos in the street.
We would retreat,
Pull back,
No longer able to repeal our lower, sad estate,
To be just dust,
Forgetting we have been renewed,
The Potter recreating,
Souls recast,
We have been changed,
Our earthly clay parts rearranged for yearning,

1. 2 Cor 4:7–18; Heb 12:1–2

Seeking after God,
The things that are above.

We are His chosen ones,
Holy,
Beloved,
More sons than sinners,
Called to speak and act
in gentleness,
In patience and humility,
To see the Truth,
And in our knowing,
Bear in mercy with the weak.

That's us—
The weak,
The ones called to forgive,
To love.

Herein lies all our stumbling.

But He,
The All Sufficient One,
Brings power to the agonies of everyday,
Reconciling all His stumbling souls to God.
His blood makes peace,
Makes us more real,
More able to withstand the suffering and pain,
More willing to reach out and love again,

More creatures for a different world,
A holy people made to claim a holy place.

His Ever—present Now
that never lets us stand alone,
But walks with us from grief to grief,
Encircling us in grace until we taste His Not Yet,
Still is shouting out His promises to pilgrims,
From the ancient cry of Adam,
To the last who wears His name and stands outside the gate.
The weary here,
Who wait with us,
The stumbling church,
Will keep on walking,
Living,
Dying,
Standing in His hope
until our earthly parts no longer feel the ache of guilt,
Or tears of shame,
But finally meet the Author,
And the Finisher,
Our Savior,
Face to face.

Unmasked[1]

People argue vigorously about the masks.
They check their social distancing at every door.
Like moral theater,
Righteous heads evangelize their science,
Reprimanding non—believers,
Preaching sermons of compliance.
Everyone believes this galloping pandemic
is the best political device
to shore up neighborhoods
from every possible persuasion,
Hoping to unseat the other side.

How wonderful
to steer this miracle of power,
Elevating self—importance and control.
How critical to choose
the right crusade,
The principled expression
that upholds what you believe
down to your very soul.

You do not drive.
Your souls are driven,

1. Matt 25:31–40; Rom 14; 1 Pet 4:8

Repeatedly displayed.

You do not see

how easily

The LORD has torn away your smug pretenses,

Stripping off the cloaking shields you use

to hide your hearts.

Can you not comprehend

you are a wound away from disaffection,

Breach of trust,

An alienation carved so deeply in your core

that you must strike against your brother,

So cruelly misaligned

that both your eyes and souls are blind?

How easily it comes to bite,

And to devour one another.

Even on our better days,

Compassion stands six feet apart,

Self—distancing ourselves from all the tangibles of grace

that He has gifted us

as we are home,

At work,

Or as we gather with each other

and before our God in prayer.

Masks are only metaphors

of what exists beneath the skin.

We wear our prophylactic wrapped around our heart and soul,

Preventing anyone from getting in.

Fear of death,

Fear of ending all alone,

Fear of hate,

Or being named as hateful,

Fear of others seeing us as wrong—

It keeps us up at night,

Deleting daring hearts that might have reached beyond ourselves,

Prohibits us from wearing someone else's coat a mile or two,

Or blocks our ears to hear the frightened cry of those with
weaker faith.

When did we see You sick,

Or locked in prison, we have asked,

So full of all compassion that we shared our fellowship?

And He has answered,

When you did it to the least of these,

My brothers,

You have done it then to me.

We are unmasked.

A Bridge of Grace[1]

Passing someone on my morning walk,
We both make space between us,
Trying to social distance.
I say,
Good morning!
With a smile,
And she is startled,
Focusing on staying clear
instead of talk.

LORD,
Help me be a cheerful neighbor.
I want to be a bridge of grace.

Christian friends are camped on either side
of wearing masks.
On whether life is liberty,
Or liberty is free to favor weaker brothers,
One conscience bending toward the other.

LORD,
Help me be a kinder, more forgiving friend.
I want to be a bridge of grace.

1. Rom 14; 1 John 4:7–21

The older neighbor made monastic,
Living in seclusion,
Conquered by her fear,
Her age,
And her infirmities,
Is separated from communities,
From energies that flow from people meeting eyes to eyes,
Touch to touch,
Meandering from thought to thought in happy talk.
Does she need groceries,
Or just a listening ear?

LORD,
Help me be a Dorcas in her life.
I want to be a bridge of grace.

Older couples,
Segregated from each other
after more than fifty years,
The one eclipsed by wandering
in mazes of his mind,
The other by a body
that has traded lively elegance
for slow,
Ungainly shuffles with a cane.
They live in different wings.
They are alone.
The one who always helped the other
now bereft.

No way to serve with pleasure in her love,
No one to be the joyful treasure of his heart.
Nothing left but vacancies and loss.

LORD,
Help me be a servant of the Cross,
A letter writer to the one who reads,
A confidant in prayer.
For You alone know what each person needs.
I want to be a bridge of grace.

Our quarantines
accentuate our separations from each other.
Is not every person made an invalid by sin?
No mask or social distancing
will stop the flow of droplets of despair,
Of shame,
Of anger,
Or of greed.
And further quarantines will
only emphasize the lonely buried deep within.
We need the Cross,
We need the humble,
Self—effacing sacrifice of Christ
to bridge the unassailable
between God's righteous paradise
and our corrupted earth.
We need His new creation of forgotten hopes and dreams,
His reconnecting tattered seams

that daily tear and fray under our isolating tendencies,
Our dark disease.

What broken people rend,
He Mends,
Is mending us,
Is calling us to bind the wounds,
To be His fellowship,
His hands and mouths of love and peace
to great and small,
To rich and poor,
To young and old,
To living, hurting people in between the times,
To intercede before the Throne
until we meet our Savior face to face,
To live and work amidst the chaos of the Marketplace,
And be His bridge.
LORD,
Help me be His bridge of grace.

A Threefold Cord[1]

May I stand beside you, friend?
You and I know
what it means to fear,
To not be in control.
Yet here we both bend
hard into the wind.
We know the storm.
We lived its furies.
We have been tattered,
Flung across the sky,
Pressed and jarred against the land.
But not alone.

He never makes us ride the gale
without His arm around us,
Or His people close at hand.

May I extend my heart to yours?
Our prayers
are shouted,
Weeping,
Pleading,
Boldly reassuring,

1. Eccl 4:9–12

Whispered in His ear.

He hears.
We are securely held,
And He will carry you and me until the end.
May I stand beside you, friend?

Tethered[1]

He knows somehow, he's not at home,
His daughter could have
helped him understand.
But she is not allowed to hug
or hold him close,
She is not given any chance
to let him know just why
his drifting mind has changed his circumstance.

Dying,
Even slowly,
Is a solitary role.
Yet we were made to travel through this awkward dance
in tandem,
Hand in hand,
A word of hope,
A friendly face,
Someone who loves us
walking on the trip as far as friends can go,
At least up to the gate.
One last embrace
before our drifting bodies
leave this weary world,
And claim another, better place.

1. Ps 90:14; Matt 26:40; Luke 22:42

Our dying
should be covered by our neighbor's love,
Among the people we have known,
And have known us.
Not singled out by protocols,
Not separated by an endless list
of antiseptic safety rules.
To be so thoroughly and firmly disconnected
from such sweet and gentle fellowship
is agony.
It underlines the lonely we already own.
It tears away the fabric of community,
The tether that belonging
graces to a fearful heart.

And thinking on the dying
I will bear someday,
Afraid I might be called to die apart,
I see my Savior,
Sorrowful and troubled at Gethsemane.
He took three friends to sit and pray with Him.
They fell asleep.
Could you not watch with me one hour?
Jesus said.
Could you not watch and pray with me a little bit?
My dying is a heavy, aching dread.
(God's cup of wrath is coming,
It will rain our wickedness upon His head.)
Remove this cup,
He prayed,

Yet not my will,
But yours, be done.

I cannot know His agony.
My own is tempered by His blood.
My walk is tethered
to His solitary journey to the Cross.
He felt abandonment.
He understood forlorn.
He knew neglect.
There is no sorrow,
No estrangement from compassion
He has not already met
and faced it down.
Perhaps I will end with a sigh,
Forgotten and companionless,
But not in fear,
And not alone.
My LORD is near.

O satisfy me every morning
with Your steadfast love,
I pray.
That I may in all things rejoice,
And be here,
Every moment,
Truly glad,
In fellowship or separation,
All my days.

Truth[1]

A bright wind blows,
Is blowing through,
A fresh, cold air,
Awakening the soul within
to see the truth,
See what is just,
See what is pure,
To truly see
realities so often hidden from our eyes.
And we,
Eyes closed,
Are dulled too often,
Unaware that Truth is passing by,
And Justice calls us in the street,
And Purity despised,
Forgotten,
Vibrant in His glorious nature fills our air,
While we retreat.

What smog,
What fetid, feted air is gathering,
Is floating everywhere?
Why are we caught up in its stench?

1. Pss 25:5, 119:160, 145:18; Phil 4:8; Jas 1:18

Oh, for a breeze,

A bright and brilliant breeze

to blow the smoke,

Remove the stink.

To be aware,

At last aware

that Truth has always been right here,

Strong,

Strident,

Fiercely standing here before our eyes,

And we weren't cold enough to blink.

God is Good[1]

God is good,
I say out loud.
I do not understand
what God has planned,
Or how divergent acts
will glorify His name,
Or bring praise to His throne above.
Somedays it is so difficult
to see His hand at work
in what is happening,
To know that nothing in this world
can separate me from His love,
Or that the sorrows that have crossed my path
are for His glory and my good.

When God moves Joseph
off to Egypt as a slave,
It looks like death.
What is this wilderness
that sells a kid,
And makes him work for someone else,
A foreigner
who does not even know his God?

1. Gen 37:12–36, 46:28–34; Jonah; Matt 12:38–41; Luke 11:32

It is a wilderness of faith
where it is better to be thought of with contempt,
A shepherd
in a world where shepherds are apart,
Exempt from public life,
A place of sacred preservation,
Prearranged,
And carefully unfolded from the start.
We see a hated son.
God sees a people much beloved.

When God sends Jonah
off to preach to those he wishes dead,
The prophet sails another way,
And ends up praying from inside
the belly of a fish.
It looks like death.
What wilderness is this
that takes a sinner down to Sheol
for three long days and nights
to bring about a greater gift?

It is a wilderness of grace
that ends a rift between a people and the LORD.
For neither prophet nor the Ninevites
are capable of making peace
without God's saving grace.
Who knows,
The people cry,

God may even now relent,

And turn away from all His fiercest wrath.

Even now we may not die.

We see an angry man against an evil foe.

God sees they all are wickedness and judgment

waiting to be slain

unless the God of Mercy reaches down

to staunch the bloody flow.

A sullen, righteous man

is struggling with the hand forgiveness named,

While all his enemies are glad that Jonah came.

When God the Father sends His Son

into a broken world,

The people do not recognize

the wonder of omnipotence

intruding into every day,

Intruding into that most sacred

Grand Embodiment of Living Word.

He taught,

He preached,

He dined,

And joined with others in the feasts.

The people ask for signs.

Their hearts,

Too hard to recognize the Son of Man.

The men of Nineveh,

Will rise up at the judgment,

Jesus says,

They will condemn such unbelief.
What wilderness is this
where God Himself is made despised,
Rejected,
And the Ninevites
are better at repenting
than the well—protected family that Joseph saved?

There will be death.

It is the wilderness of hope,
That ones so lost,
So blind,
So utterly devoid of righteousness could ever find
the radiance of glory on their heads.
Yet here we are,
Just like the Ninevites outside the favored kin,
Just like the selling brothers hoping to erase a greater son,
Unknowing that he is the one to save them all—
We stand with them.

And so,
I come around again to say that
God is good.
I still don't understand what God has planned,
Or how divergent acts will glorify His name,
Or bring praise to His throne above.
It still is difficult to see His hand
in what is happening here,

But this I know,

That nothing in this world

can separate me from His love,

And all the sorrows that will cross my path

are for His glory and my good.

The Church Cries Out to God[1]

Here we are, LORD,
Grieved by various trials,
Tested on the earth by this pandemic and its fear,
By pressures from our neighbors to abort our love for God,
To favor Here above Your glorious Word,
And then John's blessing—
Grace to you,
And peace from Him
who is,
Who was,
And is to come.

LORD, rearrange our thinking,
Redirect our hearts to worship You.
You are the One who is before all things.
For every molecule,
Each atom,
Stays where it belongs
because You hold it there.
The air we breathe,
The gravity that keeps us planted firmly
on this massive hurling ball
of water, rock, and fire,

1. Col 1:17; 1 Pet 2:8,16, 4:12–14, 16, 19; Rev 1:4–5

Winding round a flaming star,

We are sustained.

We flourish

by Your mighty power.

And You who made us and uphold us

by Your righteous arm,

You loved us,

Having freed us from our sins

by Your own blood.

Your work,

Reclaiming souls and bodies destined for the fire,

Calling wounded people out of darkness,

Out of malice and despair,

Has rescued us to glorify Your mercies with our lives.

Raise us up as holy witnesses to this old

Shouting,

Angry,

Crushing,

Soulless world,

To speak of joy in every circumstance,

To live with love

where there is only hate and grief.

To share Your hope among the dying where deep sadness thrives
and shadows creep.

To be a gathering of grace,

The hands and feet of kindness in the common thoroughfares,

Embracing lonely hearts,

And placing hands of comfort on those needing to be touched.

To make a space for just one more,

No matter what the situation bears.

To earth—bound listeners and watchers,

Those who see You as a stone of stumbling,

A rock of great offense,

Who do not know,

Who won't believe,

We ask for patience and longsuffering,

For peace to understand

that they who rile against us only scream to You through

we who hover close at hand.

And as we share Your suffering,

Increase our joy,

Our fellowship,

And help us see

that we who struggle in this difficult,

This brutish,

Short,

And painful life,

Are not alone,

Are now and for forever free,

Much beloved children of the living God,

Who have a home of grace,

Of peace,

Of endless joy for all eternity.

We Battle in Christ

You are a hiding place for me; you preserve me from trouble; you surround me with shouts of deliverance.

—Ps 32:7

To Him We Bow[1]

Praise to Him who loved us,
And has freed us from our sins by His blood.
Praise to Him,
To Him be all the glory and the power,
Now, forever, and forever,
Praise Him,
Praise His holy name.
To Him we bow.

Behold His throne!
The realm of Sinai blasts upon a
wanting world.
For who can truly stand before our God?
This is the Real that rested
sometime on a mountain,
All its blazing glory
roaring,
Lightning flashing,
Rumblings and peals of thunder.
See!
Behold as well,
The light,
The glorious rainbowed blaze of color,

1. Exod 19:16–20; Rev 4

Beauty upon beauty rising up
in glowing hues,
And I am left in wonder as
the brightest Aurora Borealis quivers,
Weaving ribboned miracles across the heavenly vaulted sky.

Behold the Royal Court!
The elders
(twenty—four),
His councilors,
His heavenly advisors
all await the living creatures,
Cherubim and seraphim,
Who,
Praising day and night
are ceaseless in their calling,
Crying out,
Holy, Holy, Holy
is the Lord God Almighty!
Flying back and forth they shout,
Who was and is and is to come!
And as they cry,
The elders,
Casting down their crowns,
Fall in obedience before the throne,
Worshipping the One who lives forever and forever.
(Who can truly stand before our God?)
And they, too, cry aloud,
Worthy are you,

You, our Lord and God,
To receive the glory,
All the honor,
All the power,
You created all that is,
And by Your will
what is,
Exists and was created.
Praise Him,
Praise His holy name.
To Him we bow.

Doxology[1]

How can I tell you who He is?
How can I possibly explain
and understand what He has done?

He is the echo in the fluttering
of wings and leaves,
His name is whispered in the air,
His hands sustain the molecules
that make what is to be,
Become.
He brings the rain,
He sifts the snow,
He weighs the dust,
And fills the cracks with life unseen.
He blows,
And mountains,
Layering their sediment and fire,
Sculpt the rocks and peaks between,
Like monuments
to all consuming power,
Lift themselves to reach on high,
To gaze upon their Maker's face.

1. Ps 148; Isa 53:3–6, 55:10–12; Rev 5

Breathing,

Bursting life in worship,

Renders teeming flocks of birds in flight

like flowing ribbons,

Waltzing in the sky to songs we cannot hear

but only see their perfect rhythm as they float and dance across
the air.

Enormous teams of racing horses,

Trampling beasts

join in the merriment,

In holy jubilation.

Even weaving shoots of green,

All growing,

Reach up eagerly

to fill up every ounce of space and share their praise,

Declaring to their cosmic Majesty,

His Kingship

in their dance to live

as He has named,

Obedient to grace His wilding world,

Domesticated by His Word,

By His commanding

Let there be!

Then there is Man,

A different creature altogether.

Meant to worship

his Creator,

Yet allowed to make a weighty choice:

For Him.

For Self.

To rule His grand dominion

as His will designed,

Or rule a thousand little dynasties,

A house of empty thrones.

Rebellion chose.

Our own ascendency arose,

Releasing

scores of human demigods to worship.

Not one soul in awe

of what so eagerly,

So rashly,

And disdainfully was left behind.

How could ones formed so lofty, be so blind?

He could have crushed us,

Every single one a mad

elusive vapor in the wind.

A Word,

A passing putrid smell,

A frown,

Perhaps a fading sound,

Was that a scream?

No.

Just the whining breathless moan

when winter wraps itself around a tree.

I thought I heard,

And then forgetting,

Just as if we'd never been,
Or had been known.

But He,
More beautiful,
More holy,
Gracious,
Merciful,
Much greater in His wisdom and His love,
Chose some of these foul creatures for His own.
Not to be slaves,
But to be sons,
And rightful heirs.

The cost to end
our gross atrocity,
To put the world aright,
Required total ruin of the Royal Son,
Demanded public shame,
Humiliation
of the One who ruled it all.
He wore our frame,
And knew the cares of earthly life.
He let our names be
flogged and carved across His back.
He took the bloody crown of demigods
and wore it as His own.
He let men nail his hands and feet,
The hands that reached to touch,

To comfort and to heal the most unclean,
The most defiled,
The feet that ran toward those
all others loathed,
That sought the scorned,
The shunned,
The most reviled.
He let men slap His mouth,
Bold lips of truth, of power, and of peace.
He took the blame,
All our blame,
And let the Father rain down
all His righteous wrath,
His dreadful judgment
on the Son,
The least deserving,
For the sake of us,
Appalling creatures,
well—deserving shattering annihilation.

Only in His sacrifice,
His blood atoned.
Our debt was paid and satisfied.
And in His death
we received His righteousness,
His Name.
The breath of Holy Kings
breathed down into the marrow of our bones,
Our inheritance as sons,

As rightful heirs renewed,
Regained.

His resurrection
promises a better way
to navigate an angry, broken world.
And as He lays a claim
for greater heaven,
Greater earth,
Our former days
are all forgiven,
Just as if we'd never owned such treachery,
Or even grieved the One
who makes what is to be,
Become.
For He,
And He alone,
Deserves our praise,
For who He is,
For what He's done.

Worthy is the Lamb[1]

Who is worthy
to reveal the contents of the scroll,
And break the seven seals?
Who in heaven or on earth
has all authority,
To carry out God's story,
Making Not My People,
Mine Forever.

Changing lost,
Forgotten,
Into loved,
His excellent and treasured ones,
In whom is His delight?
From splattered blood,
Red blood upon the lintel,
While the sanguine flow
drips down the sides,
To the reach of Calvary's goal,
Intending Cross
and broken body
to fulfill,
Where only sacrifice abides,
Where only death can be enough

1. Isa 53:4; Jer 31:33; Hos 1:9–10, 2:23; Rom 9:24–26; Rev 5

to save the treasured sons.
Only the Lamb
can satisfy the awful debt
between the Father and His own.
It's His!
It's His own blood
that carries you and me!
And only He would let them
nail His body to that bitter tree!

Can any sweeter chorus be
before such agony of love?
The Lamb,
The One who died
and rose again,
The One Who Has Redeemed,
The One who is,
Who was,
And is to come—
The scroll is His.
Worthy is He,
To take the scroll,
To open up its seals.
For He was slain,
And by His blood
has ransomed people for our God.
From every tribe,
From every nation

He has made them priests
of Him who reigns forever.
They who are My People,
They shall rule upon the earth.

New voices echo on and on
in praise before the King,
Myriads and myriads,
Ten thousand times ten thousand angels,
Singing,
Worthy is the Lamb,
The Lamb who was slain,
To receive power and wealth,
Wisdom and strength,
Honor,
Glory,
And blessing!

And growing still,
The song grows in a grand crescendo,
Even rocks and stones cry out,
The beasts and birds
in bleats and trills,
The crawling things,
The daffodils in harmonies,
The brilliant stars,
Huge fireballs of light
must shout and sing,
And bring their holy offerings.

To Him who sits upon the throne,

And to the Lamb,

Be blessing,

Honor,

Glory,

And be power now and ever and forever.

The living creatures said,

Amen!

The elders,

Twenty—four,

Fell down and worshipped once again.

Memento Mori[1]

I lift my eyes up to the hills,
What god is there?
I find that Science reigns.
She claims her pantheon,
And all the people praise her works.
The Queen of labs,
Manipulating genes,
Restructuring the elements.
(The elements another made,
Not her.)

She wields a Janus knife.
One slash brings better worlds,
And with it comes a host of unexpected consequences.
A cancer cured,
A thousand angry cuts that injures life
to bring remission on.

A vaccination serves a generation.
Illness,
With its towering energies,
Adapts,
Adjusts.

1. Pss 50:10, 121:1, 148:3; 2 Cor 5:21

82

What once has saved the day

is now a Frankenstein

Inventing,

Recreating,

Changing bug to something else.

A worthy nemesis restrains the Queen

with possibilities that never come,

And certainties that never leave.

She thinks her powers great.

She is deceived.

The god we seek is death.

And even Science,

Must admit reluctantly,

She sometimes has become death's mistress by her alchemy.

I lift my eyes up to the hills,

What god is there?

I find that hubris reigns,

Audacity and vanity its secret names.

What vain delight

to think that you and I

are capable of everything!

We climb the highest mountains,

Plumb the depths of rolling seas.

We reach for stars.

We understand dominion,

But we cannot tame the heart.

The ones who grasp at destiny

use stubborn hands and sullen feet.

For every honest word or deed
the heart amends,
Deceives itself,
Restructuring its mirror image
into something touched by hell it cannot see.
It cannot tell that metamorphosis
is rearranging proper satisfaction into pride,
The goodness in the act already shed.
The god we seek is death.
And though we walk and talk like beautiful humanity,
We are already dead.

I life my eyes up to the hills,
What god is there?
I find that money is exalted,
Glorified,
And celebrated far above so many things.
It is the god of Things.
Things of comfort,
Things to wrap around ourselves
to say we beat the odds.
We are okay,
We are above the fray,
We have arrived.

A robust bank account
is better than an empty hand,
We say,
And wink.

It pays the bills.

We do not mind some economic poverty,

At least the picture that we are in unity

with those who work with less.

We like to share,

A contribution here and there.

It gratifies a conscience worried by

a vaguely floating worship of the things we wear or buy

to decorate our world.

No car,

No home,

No scrap of cloth can save a soul.

It does not even satisfy.

For one good dress deserves another,

And a pair of shoes.

What gains are these?

What do we lose?

So easily disdained and spurned for better things,

Replaceable commodities

so easily displaced,

So easily abused or burned.

Our enemy is not a lack of plentiful supply.

There never is enough to feel complete.

The god we seek is death.

And we who worship here

have sold ourselves for pennies on the street.

I lift my eyes up to the hills,

What God is there?

The God who made the heavens and the earth.

The God who made the elements

with which the Queen of Science plays.

The God deserving all the glory,

All the power,

All the praise.

Every beast that roams the forest,

This God says,

Is mine,

The cattle on a thousand hills,

No living creature lives and breathes outside His holy will.

He knows our hankerings,

Our careless,

Deadly cravings

for so many lesser gods.

He knows our loneliness,

Our fear,

And our despair.

He knows and loves.

He cares.

For our sakes

He was made our vanity,

Our gross iniquity.

(He knew no sin.)

He bore the raging fires of our dark hypocrisy,

And turned our crass futility
and faithless worshipping
to dust and ash.
He died.

And He who died
is now the One who lives!
And we who died and are now alive through Him,
Are also raised!
The God we seek is life!
And He has promised us that He
will walk with us,
Will lend His faithful presence as we struggle on this earth.
He is our shield in trouble,
And His hand
our guide from death into eternity.

Do not forget.

I lift my eyes up to the hills.
One death,
His death alone
has turned our death toward everlasting, sacred hope.

Christus salvator meus!
He who took our death
has brought us into endless life,
Remember Christ.

Upended Feast[1]

Death is there,
It always has been there,
Lurking in the shadows,
Sometimes embracing whole communities.

Good neighbors laboring together
to create a garden,
To exert dominion over weeds and over chaos,
Wake one day
to find that one is left,
The other taken.

Some are philosophical.
The man was old.

Others cry and plead,
My son, my son!
Why did you feel the need to take my son?

But everywhere is fear.
Fear of loving,
Fear of living,
Fear of Being,

1. Ps 141:7; Isa 5:14, 25:8; 1 Cor 15:24–26; 2 Tim 1:10

Fear of ending up alone.

This shadow can steal anyone.
It does not care.
It will not spare the poor,
The weak,
The rich,
The strong.
Eventually they all are gone.

So, we have conjured gods
and worshipped them
to hold death back,
The gods of
Comfort, Safety, and Security,
Warm blanket gods,
Deities of coziness,
Of cheerful reassurance,
Soothing beings borne from vast imaginations
believing they could keep the cold away,
Could calm our restless fears.
A grand abandonment of reasoning
to think that wishing,
Masks and distancing,
Making safer spaces,
More controlled and crafted neighborhoods
could overcome the Great Inevitable,
The final breath that separates
our purposefully,

Charging,
Never—ending race to greet our end.

One Man,
One God,
The Son,
The Christ,
The Lamb,
Embodied in one form—
He is the only mend.

He wore our frame.
He understood our fear.

He recognized that death devours sinners,
Eagerly partakes of our unholiness,
Our wild rebellious hearts,
Savoring the flavors of irreverence,
Dishonesty,
And guilt—
The very essence of our thoughts,
Our deeds,
Of us,
We who would stand impertinently before a holy God.

This Man/God
knew the only way
to take away death's gorging mouth,
Was serve Himself up as the feast.

He lived the way we cannot live.

He offered up His body in our place.

He let the true God,

God, the Father,

Rain our ruin,

All our terrible disgrace upon the Son.

Thirsting, hungry death

engorged himself

on One who wore our human shame as if His own,

And yet this God/Man had no guilt.

The Perfect bore the ruthless brunt (that we deserved)

to satisfy God's holy zeal.

He became the monster.

He,

The meal.

And in Christ's offering,

The heady fragrances of peace

arose before the throne.

The enmity between a people

and the God of heaven,

Met its final swallowing,

The final gulp that separates

our purposefully,

Charging,

Never—ending race to greet our end

was overshadowed,

Scattered,

Death forever shattered in a thousand times ten thousand bits of dust,

Then swept away.

And in Christ's resurrection,
Death no longer carries sway,
No longer steals.
Death,
A waning shadow,
Knows his time is racing toward his own demise.
His own upending,
When his empty promises of peaceful ends
will be revealed as vacant fantasies,
As haunting cries.

Death,
The Eater,
Eaten up by immortality,
By the splendor of Christ's dazzling Day!

And in that Day,
Good neighbors laboring together,
Will work amidst His garden,
On their lips such gratitude,
Ten thousand times ten thousand songs of gratitude
in honor of His sacrificial meal!
And all will worship Him,
And praise His holy,
Never—ending,
Boundless grace
which has no end!
Forever and forever we will sing,
We will proclaim,
Amen! Amen! Amen!

The Horsemen[1]

The Adversary wanders back and forth
upon the earth.
Pacing up and down,
Searching,
Seeking prey,
Crouching at the door
to tame the church,
To neuter truth,
To bring an end to righteous victory.

And in his train,
He brings his war by any means—
Famine,
To decrease our trust in God's sufficiency.
Fear,
To hinder fellowship.
Disease,
To taunt endurance and discourage hope.
Arguments,
To focus hearts on pride, on self,
Where even sitting side by side,
We only see our distance,
Only feel our separation,

1. Ps 2:12; Job 1:7; Rev 6, 11:15

Cling more tightly to our solitude,
Our discontent,
To smother gratitude and grace.

It pleases the Seducer
if we swim in these disruptive waters,
No longer listening to hear each other
or the truth,
Despising it,
Nor recognizing
when the Word no longer speaks,
And conversation reeks
of comfortable illusions,
Pretty phrases laid in wait
to trap and crush a wasting heart.
He celebrates
at each and every
famine of the Word of God.
He revels
in a people
wandering from sea to sea,
From west to east,
A people running back and forth
in search of peace,
A people chasing everything,
Except the LORD,
Except His Word.
To such there cannot be relief.
And nations,

Plotting to relieve the Christian from his Christ,
Dispense their mad decrees,
Participate in all the horrors demons teach
to crush a church.
So many dead! the martyrs cry,
Our hearts are ground to dust.
Our sorrows bury us!
How can we reconcile
injustice done against the dead
who lived and died in Jesus' name?
Our blood cries out beneath Your altar.
At what cost will God's great triumph be revealed,
Our sacrifice be known?
How long before You judge,
Before You rise up to avenge?
We plead our cause before Your throne.

To those whose testimonies
led them to be slain,
God patiently explains,
Rest.
Rest a little longer.
Rest until the number of your sacrifice for Christ,
For Me,
Is done.
Rest until the war against the Son
becomes
The Kingdom of our LORD and of His Christ.

And to the Adversary,
And the kings of earth—
I AM your Judge,
Your Conqueror.
While seasons come and go,
While night and day remain,
Expect My justice
to be mingled with your war.
You persecute and render pain.
I see.
You practice to deceive the ones I love.
I know.

There will be blood.
I give you up to what you are,
And let your ruthless hearts run free.

I will avenge.

You here,
Who gleefully embrace your famine,
Seek disruption,
Welcome death—
Repent while there is still a chance.
Beware the Day.
Your reckoning is coming.
Kiss the Son lest he be angry,
And you perish in the way!

Shopping[1]

What complexity
we humans are,
A constant wrestling
between the saint and sinner,
Between clean hearts attuned,
And wanderings with shooting stars,
Brightly colored packaging,
Seductions,
Calling out,
Enticing,
A Mardi Gras of promises,
A thousand lies delighting to be found,
Be canonized,
The Great Almighty Satisfy.

Why follow what cannot abide,
What cannot last?
What solid ground is there
when permanence is
drifting,
Shifting,
Changing,
Choosing various commitments by the hour,

1. Prov 1:20–33; 1 Cor 6:19–20

Safety not defined by truth,
But by my comfort or your power?

Wisdom, too,
Cries in the streets.
Speaks a marketplace of truth.
Too many do not hear.
Too many,
Caught by pleasures,
Momentary lights and quick distractions,
Noisiness and bother,
Find only rusting treasures,
Broken bits of fading hope
that cauterize,
That flash and melt,
And then,
Like jaded mistresses,
Despise and spurn.

Beware!
You are the merchandise,
The window dressing,
One of many items on display.
You thought you were the beauty,
You're the beast.
You thought you were the buyer,
You're the feast.
Many eagerly would pay to own your heart
and give you up to burn.

Only God can break a heart,

Can disengage the tangles of deceit,

Can disengage the sinning from the saint

and make a better Man.

Unless the Holy Spirit

whispers in your ear,

And draws you in

to see more clearly

what is real and what is not,

You cannot know.

You cannot be the best of you,

Or find the safest place.

The best is to be captured,

Bought,

By One who loves.

For only He

is willing to pay everything,

Go all the way to death,

And lose Himself,

A cosmic bartering—

One sacrifice in blood for many souls.

Unless He buys,

You cannot choose the saint,

Or let the sinner die.

You cannot find true peace,

Be recognized and loved,

And kill the Lie.

Holy War[1]

Lord, give me strength
to do Your will.
I would do good.
I would be kind.
I struggle here with fear.
I am afraid.
And sometimes overwhelmed
by all the violence this world sanctifies and bears.
I am an exile in a wilderness of strife,
An anxious neighbor to an angry crowd,
And I am bowed
by my own sin as well as theirs.

I walk a wilderness of pain,
A wilderness of faith.
A daily trudging through the sand and underbrush,
The sharp and stinging plants,
The desert wind,
The heat,
The pressing need for nourishment and water,
Shelter.
Sometimes struggles are within,
Sometimes without.

1. Gen 3:15, 11:3–4; Jer 31:2; Rev 12

This is my war.

His war, too.

It was His war before my own.

There is a churlish dragon stumbling out,

The Lord of Outrage,

Prosecutor of my thoughts and deeds.

He is dark havoc,

Settled in the city like a fog of doubting and despair.

He oozes shame,

And tries to cloud his smoke and fumes

around the people living there.

Confusion,

Anger,

Hatred follows where he reigns.

He would have swallowed up Messiah,

But the Emperor will not allow such mercenary power

to find its total rule.

God's arm restrains.

The weaponry of God's own choice is sacrifice and suffering.

God's sacredness must be abused

to overcome such miserable intent.

His heel is bruised.

The churchy people do not recognize the Son.

They hate His words.

Their empty souls are stung by truth's rebuke.

They are undone,

And hearts already roiling smoke and fumes prefer His death,
Not knowing they have sealed their own demise,
Unless His scandalizing sacrifice,
His blood,
Is scattered on their own depravity,
Is scrubbed across their charnel lives.
There is no other way to make amends,
No safer,
Kinder road.

Love is a dagger to the heart of He who knew no sin.
Love bears the pain.
Love lets the wrath of heaven enter in.
Love counts it gain.
Love's agony reverses human blasphemy, and clinging shame.
In doing so,
The cruel deceiver
can no longer prosecute,
His claims cannot indict.
For Right has riven death in two,
Has ripped audacity and crass rebellion into shreds.
The dragon no longer stands to scream the guilt of God's beloved,
To bend tormented heads.
This dragon now is flung,
Flung down to waste upon the earth,
Thrown down to harry war against the church.

Lord, give me strength

to do Your will.

I would do good.

I would be kind.

I struggle here with fear,

I am afraid,

And sometimes overwhelmed

by all the violence this world sanctifies and bears.

I am an exile in a wilderness of strife,

An anxious neighbor to an angry crowd,

And I am bowed

by my own sin as well as theirs.

I walk a wilderness of pain,

A wilderness of faith.

A daily trudging through the sand and underbrush,

The sharp and stinging plants,

The desert wind,

The heat,

The pressing need for nourishment and water,

Shelter.

Sometimes struggles are within,

Sometimes without.

It is God's wilderness that conquers me,

That gives me hopeful energy to carry through,

That holds the dragon back.

It is His blood that covers me,

Embodies what I lack,

Even to death,

That stills the dragon's voice,

Erasing every

whispered,

Damning sigh and groan.

This is my war.

His war, too.

It was His war before my own.

More Than Conquerors[1]

The air I'm breathing everyday
is saturated with the smells of cultic life,
An earthly faith that counterfeits the Real.
There is an appetite for finding sinners,
Marking out the penalties required to atone,
Confession,
Asking for forgiveness,
Immediate deliverance with recompense,
Appeasement to the gods of Man,
The gods of crime du jour
(it varies day to day),
And none can say if they are truly saved.
Another day,
Another god might recognize another sin,
And all the people gathered in
will nod their heads,
And press the evildoer out the door.
Who are these gods?
What gives them power to decide our fate?
How can we overcome the horrifying weight of this?
An earthly hell
decided by our neighbors,
They who mirror image our own weaknesses and stumbling,

1. Josh 5:13–14; Isa 26:9–12; 2 Thess 2:1–12; Rev 13

They who stand up,
Screaming, *Crucify!*
So easily assenting to our social execution,
To our damning separation
from community and life?

Let us make bricks,
The god—full people say,
Come, let us build ourselves a city and a tower.
Build our name,
Praise ourselves and our abilities.
How tall the tower?
All the way to touch the sky!
We are unlimited, of course,
A glorious force
that overcomes all obstacles.
Who needs a lesser god when I am he?
Who needs a church,
When we are gathering consensus,
Building fresh theology
from vast cooperative demands.
We are the pinnacle of augury,
And ride an epic throne of power,
Re—creating,
Crafting tower after tower,
Making Babel out of dreams remembered,
Drifting smoke and shadows,
Bits of odd offenses,
Lost desires cast and recast,

Fashioned,

Gilded for a lost menagerie of man adrift.

And we would build a rift between all hearts and God.

Beware the men of lawlessness,

Inciting foolish heads to curry violence

for hollow hope that burns and dies.

They speak of justice.

There is none.

These men are grifters,

Mesmerizing talking heads.

In every mouth are words on words on words.

On every heart are printed lies.

And in this bewildering, deceptive wake,

The search for sacrificial lambs competes

with rationality and peace.

And God's beloved,

The children of the rightful King,

Are all too often

trampled underneath.

Beware of prophets,

Harbingers of fraud and proper thinking,

Always ready in the wings,

To offer ex cathedra

Sacred Oracles

(expect exciting signs and wonders),

Capturing our loyalty,

Creating cultural conformity.

The seer sings,
This is the moral thing to do.
And every listener agrees,
And says, *Amen.*
And fractured,
Strangled,
Almost Truth,
Is bled away,
And in its place,
The smell of rancor rises to
a ripening stench that rots veracity,
Revealing sham.

For earthly truth is flexible,
Is malleable,
And can be bent whichever way the
information must be compromised
to match the dragon's dark design.
For his desire is to steal the nodding souls of Man,
And vilify the people of the Lamb.

The air I'm breathing everyday
is saturated with the smells of cultic life,
An earthly faith that counterfeits the Real.
But we are priests and prophets of the LORD.
Our lives, our words,
Even our deaths, speak volumes to a hurting world.
It is the LORD who has completed all our glorious works.
They are not ours, but His.

It is the LORD who makes us able to discern what eager
    neighbors miss.

It is the LORD who opens up our eyes to see that
    sacred judgments

come with wrapping paper, bows and invitations to embrace
    the Father's love,

To truly know the LORD, and learn His righteousness revealed.

It is the LORD who died outside the camp,

It is the LORD who faced an earthly hell decided by
    His neighbors,

They who mirror image our own weaknesses and stumbling,

They who stood up,

Screaming, *Crucify!*

And easily assented to his execution.

These, from every neighborhood,

They did not see the powerful, definitive atonement they
    were searching for

was right there on that bleeding tree.

And we, His present—day ambassadors,

Might find ourselves in prison,

Martyred for a greater cause than inconsistencies

or worries that the world has disinherited its own.

We all are disinherited outside of Christ,

We all are lost,

The marginalized from hope and grace.

It is the LORD who sanctifies and makes things whole.

For Him we have been called,

To serve,

To spread abroad the Truth,

No matter what the suffering.

And we, like Joshua

(still unaware,

Still questioning just what we hear and see),

Might stand one day and ask,

Are you for us or for our foes?

And He who loves us will reply,

No! I command the army of the LORD.

Take off the sandals from your feet.

For every place you walk is holy ground.

You are with me.

Bending[1]

This world has always been a great seducer,
Asking me to bend a little,
Just a little bit
toward apathy,
Toward virtuous neglect of people.
How sad to see so many live this way.
What can I do?
I signal that I care,
A costless gesture from a wandering heart.
But who would dare to risk
the time,
The energy,
The sacrificial love required here to do my part,
To move my hands and feet,
To give my time and money to those people over there?

The world has always been a great seducer,
Asking me to blend a little,
Just a little bit
toward grand acceptance.
Everything and everyone.
No separating generous love
(without a hesitation)

1. Matt 6:19–20, 16:26; Rev 17,18

toward the one who needs,

From gentle reservations,

Words and prayers of truth

that could speak God's unending grace,

And His forever mercy,

Far beyond what I could give or tell.

Even now,

Thoughts and deeds are binding friends and family

toward God's vast eternal wrath.

Am I afraid too much to speak,

To face the persecution here,

When they who revel in their sins

are facing endless worlds of hell?

The world has always been a great seducer,

Asking me to bend a little,

Just a little bit

toward soft prosperity,

Toward getting too complacent

with the status quo,

The stuff I am devoted to,

Accumulating this and that

'til even I don't know how much I own.

Inch by sacred inch

I find I'm clinging

to the starkest,

Most harrowing idolatry.

Why do I trust in stuff?

What acquisitions do I love too much to lose?

Without the Cross,
The things I own are dust.

Come out from her,
My Savior cries,
Come out from Babylon,
Be separated from her sins!
For where your treasure is,
Your heart begins its roving search to be content.
You will not ever find it under dragon wings,
Or other useless things,
But in the arms of He who rescued you,
Who carries you,
And brings your life to holy rest.

The nations that adore the wonders of seduction,
All the temporary glories that abundance brings,
The stories that regale how powerful to be
the queen of everything,
Too easily assent to greedy mobs
who live and die by boasting,
Gloating.

Smell the ruthless wind that blows in from a viper's nest!
And from such arrogance,
How delightfully depraved,
They brag,
How decadent to drink down to the dregs
the blood of saints,

The blood of those who would not bend a knee
before the kings and priests of our rapacious immorality,
Before the worshiping of sex and stuff.

It is enough!
The Beast will scream,
Will kill the prostitute of power.
Alas,
Great Babylon is gone!
For in a single hour she will be laid waste.
And there will be no longer
any taste of all that worldly culture craves.
No more the craftsman at his craft.
No more the lamp to light the day,
Or mark the rhythm of society at work or play.
No more.
For they who worshiped power,
They who worshiped self and all its passions
far above the LORD,
Will be destroyed.
The deepest,
Darkest pit of death
is God's most holy judgment
and their beggared goal.

What does it profit anyone
to gain this passing world,
To bend a little bit too far and bow to folly and corrupt control,
To not accept the holy rescue offered up,
And lose their everlasting soul?

Just Ask[1]

Chants and slogans shouted in the summer sun,
A crash of broken glass is slivering and chopping up the dark
as arson lights a stream of angry messages
that splash across a crowded street.
What can be said
by cooler heads when raging rolls,
And ripples like a thousand waves from heart to mouth,
From mouth to eager hands and feet?
Or how can any peace be carried back across
a sea of feelings cresting overhead?
Peace, peace.
There is no peace,
The prophet said.

It's easy to get caught up in the wind
that blows in from a desert,
Loaded with contentious thoughts
that only brings more heat and tension
to a world already wearied by disease and sin.
Our politics,
Our fear of someone else's views,
The stories constantly repeated in the daily news
can blow out fortitude,

1. Jer 6:14; Luke 11:9

Or dampen joy.
Despair would rather settle us
like brittle, yellowed leaves
that crunch and shatter underfoot,
And clutter up the earthen floor.
The smell of death is in the air.
The spirit of distrust and hate is everywhere.

Where is the grace,
The patient heart pursuing Truth
that stands on what is sure,
That runs toward love,
That bears all things,
Believes,
That hopes,
And in that hoping still endures?

That grace is Christ.
That love is His for us,
And He is ready
to abundantly bestow
His generous hope and joy.
How can we possibly clear out the fog
that binds our hearts,
That would destroy,
Unless we seek,
Unless we reach and ask for Him
to rescue us in times of need.
Ask,

He says,
And I will give.
Seek,
And you will find Me true.
Knock,
And I will open up to you My mercies
on a quarrelling,
Rough and stressful day.
In every way He brings us life.

He brings us strength
for all the mundane strewn across our ordinary daily walk,
From dirty dishes,
Through to where an angry word flies hot and tempers fray,
To piles of never—ending laundry,
Met by never—ending bills,
The sort of commonplace banality that could obscure a
    proper view.

He brings us peace.
He stills our restless hearts
and calms us when we feel afraid.

He brings us joy
when we've forgotten just how much
His lavish love has dressed our lives,
And we are wondering how will this that I am going through
    work out?
How possibly can I get through today?

Yet, there it is—
Surprising joy,
Filling each of us with endless,
Growing hope
where there was none before.

And in the middle of the chaos,
In the middle of the fires of rebellion,
All the vast uncertainties,
The hate,
The violence that keeps twisting people toward despair,
He opens up a glorious door,
And all His strength,
His peace,
His love,
His endless joy comes rushing through
and clears the air.

In the Battle[1]

Law is gone,

And all her prophets find no vision in the LORD.

What kind of place is this?

What kind of people gather here?

Their anger fierce,

Their restless hearts demanding,

Crying justice,

Shouting unrelenting bitterness.

Resentment is their exercise,

Their play.

There is no peace,

No rest,

No hope,

No God.

Their troubles trouble me.

I feel their fear.

It rises up.

It seeks to rip my certainty away.

You are right here.

In everything I do,

In everywhere I go,

And I am never,

1. Lam 2:9b, 3:22–26, 5:16

Ever,

Far from peace,

Never all alone.

Not my own,

I am forever held by You.

Your steadfast love is never ceasing,

And Your mercies never end.

Every morning I am raised,

I am renewed,

I am restored to comprehend Your truth,

Your comfort.

Send me forth to battle

with the trials You have sent.

Righteous combat

overcomes a struggling heart.

With sacred trust in You,

I do repent of all my hubris,

All my vanity of soul

that would assume I had control,

That I could change this broken world,

Or rearrange the stark disorder of this place.

You are my portion, LORD,

I hope in You.

I wait in silence,

Listening for Your Word,

For Your salvation.

What would You like for me to do?

Storms[1]

Restless winds
blow in
on troubled thoughts,
Their pacing
races back and forth,
An anxious dance,
A wearing down
of any fragile peace that wraps a wrestling mind.

Who thought the winds
would blow like this?

The leaves of controversy
tumble into ever—moving
fluid piles.
They whirl in endless circles,
Old and useless arguments,
Words rehearsed and countered,
Ideas spinning,
Gathered,
Swept,
But never gone.
My thoughts go on and on

1. Isa 51:16, 52:7; Luke 21:15; John 13:1–21; Heb 1:11–12

but I am never free.
Why did I think that rest
could yet exist for me?

I am the storm.
I am the whistling harmonies of pain.
I am the roiling wind
that drags the dirt,
That stomps and pouts in royal tantrums,
Making bright,
Alluring promises
with flashing lightning strikes,
And then forgets the rain.

Give ear, O LORD.
Please hear my prayer.
Listen to my plea for grace.
I need Your rain.
I need the drenching glory of Your favor.
LORD, anoint my head,
And let its oil run down on my face.
How else can I withstand the wind?
How else can I restrain my heart from fear
or push my anxious thoughts away.

He reaches down to wash my feet.
What rain is this?
What washing rushes to my heart
by scrubbing my most ignominious parts?

And He says,

Peace!

In My blood you are already clean.

Give Me your storms.

Give Me your mind,

Your hands,

Your feet.

My glory has already been released

to guide your anxious thoughts.

I have already put My words into your mouth,

And I will give you wisdom in that day

when you are called to speak.

How beautiful

could be your feet,

If they would bring good news to men

instead of worrying how properly your words defend My name.

You are already mine.

You are already free.

Man will perish.

I, forever, and for always,

Will remain the same.

Rest in Me.

The Fields are White with Harvest[1]

Hard times,
Hard times, O Lord.
So tired, Lord.
Sometimes this world
just wears me down.
My heart is heavy for Your people
lost in pain and suffering.
Press on.
Press on.
How can I press on?
Running back and forth to marshal hope,
My spirit always running,
Leaving and forsaking all that lies behind,
Straining forward,
Reaching,
Grasping for the prize?
Pray on.
Pray on,
For You have said our prayers have power,
As You move among us,
By Your will,
Our prayers have great effect.

1. Num 13:30–33; Job 38; Psalm 103; Hab 2:20; Rom 5:1–5; Phil 3:12–14; Rev 7

And then I see this world,

Its frown devouring inhabitants with fear,

Its public words and actions

rising up to frightening heights like giants,

Like Nephilim against Your Word.

Here I stand,

A grasshopper,

An easy prey before the onslaught of disease,

Of violence,

Of lies on lies intending to deceive.

Who can I trust?

How can my worried heart believe?

And He says,

Come to Me.

Your works to overcome

can never set you free.

Without My blood,

My works,

My power,

Your works are never done.

You are a grasshopper, my friend.

Like grass and flowers,

Flourishing,

Grass and brilliant petals reaching

fervently in praise before My name.

Such fame is glorious.

Such glory fades.

The time to honor Me is brief,
Too brief
before a shriveling wind upends.
It buries you,
It buries them.

And then I ponder,
Where was I when God spoke all Creation into life?
Commanding morning,
Giving sleep
since night began?
Choosing me before all ancient times
to be His own?
He counts the birds that fill the skies.
He claims the deep,
And holds the ocean waves in place.
He separated steppe
from rolling hills,
And raised the earth to craggy peaks.
I am too fragile to hold back the dark,
Or comprehend what lies ahead,
Or change the course the sun must travel dawn to dusk.
I cannot make my troubles mend.
I might as well be seed and husk.

God alone
is holding back the end
until His people all are safely gathered in.
Behold! says John,

A multitude of nations,
Tribes,
Of peoples, and of tongues,
Are standing there, before the Throne,
Before the Lamb.
From Age to Age,
He has been gathering
a harvesting of grace,
A people captured by His love and mercy,
Sheltered,
Waiting for the End of Days.
He sees.
He knows His children's suffering and pain.

Rejoice in suffering, Jesus says.
Let Me produce endurance in your pain.
Let character grow strong and vigorous roots,
To rid the soul of weeds and weaknesses,
Revealing hope,
The hope my leaving and forgetting strived to find,
The hope that only comes
from leaning on Him all the time,
Entrusting all my life to Him,
His blood,
His sacrifice,
His suffering to get me home.

Lord, I truly am of small account,
But loved so much.

I shut my mouth.

Be still my soul.

The God of heaven is at hand.

Let all mortal flesh keep silence,

And in fear and trembling stand.

Psalm for a Difficult Day[1]

I grieve for evil's offering.
It stings,
And buries all the graces that a life could give.
What recompense could cover up such ruthlessness,
Could end destructive,
Mad despair,
Or brings true justice to the land?

Surely injustice floods and flows,
Where foes of righteousness can trample on the truth.
Where violence
is conquering,
Oppressing all our efforts,
All our gifts of kindness or our care.
Tell me,
Where are protectors,
Where the upright woman or the man?

Mourn,
Weep as sorrows rise,
As base iniquity prowls and seeks.
Speak of God's forgiveness in the face of human sins.
If You kept a record of all our transgressions,

1. Pss 88; 130:1; Isa 64:8

Dear God,

How could anyone stand?

How shall I live then before my neighbor?
Laboring,
Grateful before my LORD?
Humble my heart with Your infinite wisdom,
Grant us Your rest in the shadowlands.

Plug Yourself Into the Vine[1]

Some graffiti covers up my neighbor's wall—
God won't give you
more than you can handle here.
I stop to smile.
It sounds so clear.
It sounds so perfectly religious,
Fitting slogan for a carefully protected, churchy heart.
It does not even touch the truth.

Where do I start?
God gives me more than I can handle every single day.
He wants me leaning into Him.
He wants me gripping tightly to
His Word,
His people,
Learning as I lean,
In everything,
To choose Christ first,
To set my mind on things that are above,
Not on the things of earth,
To gain compassion,
Kindness,
Patience,

1. John 15:1–5; Col 3:22; Jas 1:2–3

Meekness,

And humility,

To put on love.

You would not think the threat of drowning

in the cares and troubles of this life

would bring about these lovely traits,

Would trade my sour, selfish side for states more beautiful,

More gracious with more depth,

More sweet,

And I would gather wisdom in the sorrows,

In the pain,

And in the crumbling times I stumble in defeat,

But there it is.

Do not be surprised

when fiery trials come your way,

Says Peter.

Count it all as blessings from above.

Count it joy,

Says James,

When you meet up with various troubles,

Knowing that they test your faith,

They build a soul of steadfastness,

A strengthened heart that will endure.

And I remember Jesus saying,

Plug yourself into the Vine.

Hold tight to Me.

I am the source of everything you need.
I may just be one solitary branch,
But when I plug myself into the Vine,
I am secure.

And when I lean,
I find His gentleness
to give the softest answer when the world is crushing down
and everything is lost.
And when I lean,
I find His strength
to make it through another day
when even dealing for an hour
seems too difficult a task.
And when I lean,
I find His peace
to manage through when stress and fear
are far too much to take an ordinary step.
It's all I ask,
I plead.

He knows me better.
I, the weak and fragile branch,
Am reaching up eternally
because I need His help in everything.

But that is what He wants,
An eager branch that clings and holds on tightly to the Vine,
An eager branch that leans in close

to gain the grace that flows from Him into my life,

And turns my living for myself into a fruitful offering.

And so, I say to you, again,

Plug in.

Plug yourself into the Vine.

Jars of Clay[1]

COVID digs by harrowing,
Its fiercest teeth are plowing through
our covenants with death,
Our covenants that honor kings above all else,
That rest in shelters
we have fashioned out of us,
Constructed out of narratives that put our egos first.
We are a constant chattering,
A gathering of birds,
A murmuration mumbling the ancient lies
as if our chittering could muzzle sacred words.

But we can never silence Truth.

And God would rather silence us for greater good,
Our greater good.
His winnowing is digging out our worst,
Removing stones
that would have crushed our love.
He'd rather let the ravens eat the tangling weeds
that could have choked our praise and prayer,
That would have swallowed up our hearts in hopelessness.

1. Isa 28:14–29; 2 Cor 4:8–9, 16–17

He cares too much
to let us wallow in the cares
that often suffocate our day.

COVID—19 simplifies.
It clears the lies.
It weighs priorities,
It helps us throw away the weightless busyness
that keeps our hearts from His.
And this we say,
While burdened with our COVID quarantines and masks:
We are afflicted, but not crushed.
Perplexed, but never driven to despair.
More and more we see our brothers persecuted,
Not forsaken.
Shaken,
Some even now struck down.

They never are destroyed.

Our COVID home is not our end.
We have a better building,
All these trials shaping hungering for holiness and heaven.
While we wait,
He gives the grace to conquer daily tasks.

He does not thresh our souls forever,
Neither will He crush.
For this is momentary,

Light affliction,

Created to prepare us for eternity,

To wean our souls from lesser things,

The weight of glory only brought to permanence by suffering.

The Watchers[1]

We're in the battle now.
It's not enough to claim some things are true
unless God's Word,
Recited week by week,
Is changing you.

We can't be watchers,
Merely watchers sitting in the pew,
Intoning creeds and verses,
Mumbling the hymns.
It can't be only words.

The world is wordy, too.

It cultivates,
It elevates and chants thoughts endlessly,
Inserting fear on fear
between the lines.
I know that dread.
It rises,
Full of drama,
Ruthlessly upending,

1. Ps 91:1–15; John 6:68; Rev 8–9

Plundering complacencies,

My sanctuaries.

All my taut security

is flattened,

Scorched

by anxious, trampling words.

We cannot live in fear of fire,

Or flashing, burning stars,

Whose fading majesties plunge ruthlessly from heaven down to
earth,

Or plagues of locusts swarming to destroy.

Apollyon,

That ancient Serpent,

Seeking to confound,

Confuse,

Is withering the world with wretched words,

With sorceries

of smoke and sulphur,

Lying,

Lying,

Trying to abuse belief,

Trying to release a carnage of distortion,

Advertising cold despair,

A coat of sanguine colors,

Dripping slander,

Meant for lost, deluded souls to wear.

We can't be watchers,
Merely watchers sitting in the pew,
Intoning creeds and verses,
Mumbling the hymns.
It can't be only words.

We who cry out,
Holy, Holy!
Stand sequestered,
Sheltered in His shadow,
Gathered to His dwelling place,
His refuge,
Covered by His blood,
His sure salvation,
Bound into the battle,
Now before His face.

To whom, said Peter,
Shall we go?
To whom indeed.
There is no other hope but Him.
You have the words of life,
Eternal life.
I quite agree.
There is no other route to take,
No course to choose.
His road before us marks our way.
It may hold sorrow.
He has carried it before we even reach for dawn.

It may be overflowing with frustration,
Hard to move,
To breathe,
To deal with pain.
He gives the strength to carry on.

His words are true.
His words are living,
Molding us,
Transforming us before His presence,
Raising us to travel far beyond
this battle—weary world of strife.
We can hold on.

He is the Word.
We are His doers,
Doing Word in trust,
By faith.
We are His arms,
His feet,
His mouth of comforting and peace
before a broken world.
We speak,
We love,
We walk where others fear to tread.
We sing His resurrection grace among the dead.
And as we do in Jesus' name,
We are the watchers,
Watching as He brings the rising,

Praising in the risen Son,

Where words and creeds,

Where elements of bread and wine

before us

turn from words

to living,

Breathing flesh and bones,

Thus ending fear,

And bringing joy

to living stones.

On Standing at the Crossroads[1]

I am not my own,
It has been said.
Yet,
Sometimes I push hard against the goads.
I want my way,
My world,
My own agenda in my time.

I fool myself.
There is no time that's truly mine.
I'm at the pleasure of the King
who welcomed me,
Who bore my craving need for fire,
My love of dark,
My wanting for desire,
Drama tempering my every breath.

He bought my death.
He took the penalty my wants deserved.
His corpse became my corpse,
His victory, His rising from the dead,
My life.
He said He'd always walk with me,

1. John 16:33; 1 Cor 6:19–20; 2 Cor 4:5–6; Rom 5:1–11

He'd never leave.

He said the road would be a rugged, anxious path,

A battleground of strife.

He said I would forget and sometimes fall,

But He would always be there,

Right beside me,

Lifting me to stand where I could only crawl.

He knows it all.

What can I do?

I live to serve.

Autonomy, I throw you down again.

LORD,

Do not let me choke the glory from Your grace.

For I, who know the excellencies

of Your divine affection,

Who have been full known,

And yet much better loved—

I need You now.

I once again must travel on the road You choose.

Must trust,

Must follow yet again Your holy will,

Not mine.

I here decline again,

I here defer my way

for Your own sacred kingdom's sake.

LORD help me

press on forward,

Keep on walking,

Keep on letting You decide the path to take.

Re—Creation[1]

Peel away,
See me as I am,
Pretenses gone.
The celebrated outer cloak
I wore each day,
It does not fit me anymore.
Experienced in vibrant colors once,
Now faded by the constant years of use.
They could be rags
if measured by the words and works I wrote.

What shall I wear for covering?

Who can I be,
But daughter of the King?
And as His Bride,
The linen He has sewn
is woven in His blood
with golden threads of love.
His robe becomes my own,
A glorious wedding dress,
More beautiful than any multicolored coat.

1. 2 Cor 5:17

Our Victory in Christ

No longer will there by anything accursed, but the throne of God and of the Lamb will be in it, and his servants will worship him. They will see his face, and his name will be on their foreheads. And night will be no more. They will need no light of lamp or sun, for the Lord God will be their light, and they will reign forever and ever.

—Rev 22:3–5

Lord of the Harvest[1]

The Harvest of the Grapes

Sons of Adam,
Daughters of Eve,
You who despise the Truth,
Refusing to bow down before the Holy King—
You can no longer rain contempt
on those for whom His blood was shed.
You can no longer practice to deceive both rich and poor,
Both small and great.
You can no longer smell or taste of sin,
Or render hate,
Or with the power of the Beast,
Divide the living from the dead.

Fallen, fallen is Babylon!
And she who claimed dominion over all,
And you who made all nations
drink the wine of her adultery,
You now are dangerously close to drinking all God's cup
of wrath—
The mug already poured,
Your sins arraigned,

1. Isa 63:3; Phil 2:11; Col 1:21–22; Rev 14:1–15:4

Your insurrections damned,

Your reservations made for fire and sulfur

in the presence of the holy angels and the Lamb—

Fear God!

Repent while there is time!

Give Him the glory.

Worship Him alone.

The sickle at the ready

soon will cut,

Will harvest all the fruit of wickedness.

And you who trampled holiness,

Who desecrated righteous works,

Who trod upon the blood of God's beloved,

Will be a carmine flow outside the camp,

A torrent of destruction,

Crushed beneath the winepress of the wrath of God.

The Harvest of the Grain

Sons of Adam,

Daughters of Eve,

You who are now victorious,

Restored and strengthened through His blood,

Who sing aloud the majesty

and greatness of His deeds,

Sing gloriously before the Lamb!

Sing out new songs of praise before the throne!

For you are His redeemed,

You are His sacred ones,

Beloved.

And by His grace alone

you have endured with patience and with joy.

You who were once estranged,

He has now reconciled,

He has delivered you from death.

And He who harvests,

Comes at last to take you home!

His work is done.

Shake Me Awake, LORD[1]

The angel pours God's wrath upon the earth.
And all whose minds and actions
magnify the Beast,
Are embroidered by their sores.
Then the LORD will say,
Once more,
And in a little while,
I will shake.
I will shake the heavens.
I will shake the earth.

Do I bind their festering scourge?
Do I mourn for my own wretchedness?
Knowing that His mercy and His grace
frame my identity,
Or give me worth?

Or do I curse God?

Obey the LORD and keep His covenant.
Shake me awake, LORD,
Shake me awake!

1. Ps 24:1; Isa 51:6; Hab 3:6; Hag 2:6; Heb 1:10–12; Rev 15:5–16:21

The angel pours God's wrath upon the sea.

And all the oceans become blood,

A floating corpse,

A watery grave where nothing lives.

It has become the Great Abyss.

Then the LORD will say,

Once more,

And in a little while,

I will shake.

I will shake the heavens.

I will shake the earth.

I will shake the sea.

Do I mourn the end of ocean grace?

Its splendor,

All the creatures suddenly doomed,

Erased?

Do I give thanks that God is conquering the Beast's domain?

The realm of wickedness,

And all the multitudes of evil,

Slain?

Or do I curse God?

Lean on His wisdom,

Trust His ways.

The earth is His.

Shake me awake, LORD,

Shake me awake!

The angel pours God's wrath upon the rivers,

On the springs.

His judgment on all those who shed the blood of saints.

And so, He taints the peoples' drink.

Their waters stink.

And those who trample down the church

will drink the dregs of their own blood like wine.

Let all flesh know,

That I, the LORD,

I AM your Savior and your King.

Do I grieve the evil perpetrated on our LORD's beloved?

Do I pray for mercy?

For His love?

Or do I curse God?

The prayer of a righteous man has great power.

The prayer of faith will save the sick,

Will bind the brokenhearted wounds.

Pray for those who still are wasting in their sour souls.

Pray that they might be healed this very hour.

Shake me awake, LORD,

Shake me awake!

The angel pours God's wrath upon the sun.

And in its blazing

sears the world with fire.

The sun burns hard with no relief.

Then the LORD will say,
Once more,
And in a little while,
I will shake.
I will shake the heavens.
I will shake the earth.
I will shake the sea.
I will shake the land.
Do I extoll His shade?
His covering grace?
He is the only true protection from the heated blaze.
Do I find refuge in His sheltering arms?
In all His faithful claims?

Or do I curse God?

His Word is salve to hurting hearts.
His presence,
Peace to those who need Him most.
What is already chaff will soon be ash.
And only what is His remains.
Shake me awake, LORD,
Shake me awake!

The angel pours God's wrath upon the Beast,
And on his throne.
And all his kingdom shutters into dark,
A dark that presses on each face,
A clinging mask of discontent,

Where there is only I and me.

Then the LORD will say,

Once more,

And in a little while,

I will shake.

I will shake the heavens.

I will shake the earth.

I will shake the sea.

I will shake the land.

I will shake the dark.

You who love the dark,

There is no space.

No other anything.

So hard to think,

To breathe.

You could be stone.

You are at last, and firmly planted here alone.

Will you repent?

Will you let go of everything

that just one minute past seemed all—encompassing,

Seemed greater than your walk with God?

Or do you curse His very name?

Beware. Be told.

There is no other more important than the LORD,

Whose light will soon expose

that what you thought was life,

Was Satan's throne.

Shake me awake, LORD,

Shake me awake!

The angel pours God's wrath on Man's defense.

There is no river to hold back the gathering

of armies greedy for the war,

No river to restrain their judgment waiting at the door.

Then the LORD will say,

Once more,

And in a little while,

I will shake.

I will shake the heavens.

I will shake the earth.

I will shake the sea.

I will shake the land.

I will shake the dark.

I will shake the world.

To all you lovers of this world,

You rise up eagerly to crush the church,

Inheritors of dark, demonic spirits,

Liars all assembling to strangle Truth—

You are deceived.

Can you yet separate what dragons speak from what is right,

Or are you deaf and only hearing dragon echoes

bouncing in the empty chambers of your minds?

Can you hear God in heaven anymore?

Behold,
Our LORD Almighty whispers,
I AM coming like a thief.
Blessed are those who stay awake
and at the ready when the battle comes.
Shake me awake, LORD,
Shake me awake!

The angel pours God's wrath on all that is.
In lightning and in thunder,
Heaven comes to roll up all Creation
like discarded garments.
Old and useless mantles cannot stay.
They are no longer found.
Perpetual and grandly carved,
The mountains shatter,
Ancient hills collapse,
And islands flee.
How terrible and mighty is His earthquake,
Splitting principalities and powers,
Pulling down the sky to scrape the earth,
Where even stars are torn and thrown away.
Yet even as the hailstones fall to crush all enemies,
The people say,
We curse you, God!
Let we who love the LORD be ready for
His glorious final rescue,
For that awesome Day!
Shake me awake, LORD,
Shake me awake!

The Feasts[1]

What terrifying war there is
between the Holy Trinity
and me.
I cannot even raise my eyes,
My face is pressed into the dust,
I might as well be dead.

The bread is passed,
The wine, consumed.
The Son is sacrificed,
His death becomes my sacred meal,
And I am fed,
Restored,
Redeemed,
My war undone,
The horrid stain is lifted from my head,
My gross unholiness demolished by His blood.
And in His hallowed work,
I trust myself to Him,
To His unfailing love.

To know such grace,
Such favor undeserved,

1. Rev 19: 6–21

How can I comprehend this pardon?

Snatching this old corpse from certain death to breath.

Not just to life,

But favored status.

I who smelled the putrid breezes

blowing from the tomb,

Am now the wooed

among a thousand upon thousand others captured

by His solemn ardor,

Chosen from before the womb.

I see a multitude,

And find we all are covered,

Undiscovered mercy now revealed,

And flowing down like purest water,

Washing out the deepest wound.

Our God is just.

He did not justify our sin,

But rained His righteous wrath upon the Son,

And not on us.

We are the Bride,

The Church,

The People of the Rood,

And welcomed to

The Marriage Supper of the Lamb.

Blessed are those who are invited to His feast.

Sing Hallelujah!

For the Lord, our God Almighty reigns.

And His beloved Bride is dressed,

Is clothed in finest linen,

Bright and pure,

For she is waiting for her groom in perfect rest.

There are two meals,

Two banquet tables spread

for eager diners ready for the feast.

The Groom,

The very Word of God,

Who breaks His enemies with rods of iron,

Administers His righteous judgment

on the Beast,

And on his lying Prophet,

Raining final war against the callous company

of kings and warriors,

Free and slave,

Both small and great.

He knows their hearts,

He does not hesitate to slay them with His sword.

The glorious King of Kings, and Lord of Lords

is riding through the battlefield,

His clothing dripping with the gory blood of all his foes.

The faithless dead are carrion for birds of prey.

Come birds that fly

to join the Supper of our God!

Be welcomed here to eat the flesh of kings,

The flesh of mighty men,

Of horses and their riders,

All the flesh of those who gathered to bring curses on the Lord.

Our God is just.

He did not justify our sin,

But rained His righteous wrath upon the Son,

And not on us.

They did not want the Son.

They would not kneel.

And so, there are two meals,

Two banquet tables spread

for eager diners ready for the feast.

One to find God's perfect mercy waiting to be offered to
the very least,

Rebellious sin untangled by a monstrous Cross.

The other to find perfect justice waiting to be executed,

Mockery and malice ready to be gored,

Rebellious sin untangled by a sharp, relentless sword.

The End of Dragons[1]

Did your God really say?
He said,
And human hearts
considered God a travesty,
His word a sham,
And bald distortion wore the crown.

It was the royal road to death,
The end of honesty,
The birth of hubris
and a cruel violence
that drove all mercy underground.
Beneath the earth
the blood of Abel,
Crying to be vindicated,
Spoke before an endless multitude
of sinners wounding sinners.
All were crushed beneath the Curse.

He was,
They were,
We all are dragons,
Brought into a grotesque fellowship

1. Gen 3:1; Rev 20:7–10

by he who tickled enmity
between the creatures and their God,
With a few spoken words—
(Did your God really say?)

We heard,
We saw,
We tested wrong desire until hearts were raw,
We fell.
And so, our history is marred,
Is tortured by regret,
By shame,
By grief,
By loss.

Our victory is in the Cross.
Our vindication finally will come.
The Dragon King
will be soon be thrust into the deepest hell,
Into the lake of fire burning day and night.
And he who did not fear
to whisper in our ear
and bring to us our own despair,
Will find his vicious torment,
All his dark perversity,
His horror,
Waiting there.

In the Book[1]

Earth and sky have fled
before the awesome glory of the One who reads,
Whose sacred finger trails across an open book.
The Book of Memorable Deeds
Or Not So Memorable,
Is being read.
And some man's every thought,
His every word and deed
are being now revealed.
This meager heart is balancing
his good deeds with the bad,
A bell curve distribution of a life of human sin.
He thinks he favors to the better side,
So, God should let him in.
Alas, it only takes one lapse,
One misdemeanor.
One infraction keeps the sinner out.
Suddenly aware,
This creature is inflamed.
The gnawing, gaping chasm
between this hardened son of Adam and a holy God
has steadily been growing
while the list of deeds was being named.

1. Deut 7:6–7; Matt 6:19–20, 25:23, 31–46; Rev 1:6, 20:11–15

What point is there in anger if your works make you a liar?
What point is there in cursing if your Maker's words are just?
Eternity awaits the damned.
This man was only known by deeds.
They threw him in the lake of fire.

Earth and sky have fled
before the awesome glory of the One who reads,
Whose sacred finger trails across an open book.
The Book of Memorable Deeds
Or Not So Memorable,
Is being read,
Another human named.
His every thought,
His every word, and deed
are now revealed,
Are swirling here like anxious gnats around his head,
And he is caught between
the pages of his life,
And Christ Who Sees.

He wants to be invisible,
His voice descending
into painful whispering.
He knows with stark,
Amazing clarity,
God's kindness weighs him down,
God's infinite compassion on a son so undeserving.
Who possibly could understand how many times

this Son of Adam missed the mark,

And found himself aghast at his own ragged sin,

While all the grace of heaven was imputed onto him?

But Judge is also Lamb.

The Book of Life is balanced on Christ's outstretched hands.

You are not known by deeds, He says,

But by My work.

Your name is evermore engraved within The Book of Life.

And this man knows that holy justice was revealed in blood.

For all eternity,

God's righteousness and peace have kissed.

Come precious son, the LORD replies,

And leads him to His Father's side.

You who are blessed beyond all measure,

Come, dear heart,

Come in! Come in!

Rejoice!

My kingdom was prepared for you,

And My inheritance for you, is yours to own.

The open door is beckoning,

Is leading him to walk the royal road

that wends so gently to God's right.

His whisper has become a glorious shout!

Praise be to Him who freed us from our sins,

And made us kings and priests to God!

For God Himself has claimed a people holy to the LORD,

Has chosen even me,

Each speaks
among a multitude,
So many others wrested from a fiery end!
Whatever clung to him before
is now the faintest buzzing by his ear.
Unconsciously his hands have brushed away the fading
murmurs of accusing sounds,
As further up,
And further in,
He joins the eager throng ascending,
Singing of the end of pain,
The end of guilt,
The end of doubt.

He is God's treasure,
He,
For all eternity.
What was, what is, what will be here
can never be destroyed.
And he can hear the Savior say,
Well done,
My good and faithful servant.
Enter now into my joy.

And then the royal finger
moves across the page,
Locating someone else's name.

Lift Up Your Eyes and See[1]

They broke his back.
They killed him with a bat.
They killed his son,
And left one younger hiding in the walls.
He saw.
He heard.
LORD,
Keep his soul from wandering,
Don't let the horror that he witnessed
lock his mind away,
But open up his crippled heart
to see Your glory written in his pain,
To know Your tender mercies will sustain.

Worn down,
She is worn down.
Her husband's body buried underground.
She runs a tendered hand
across his stone.
This missing pulls her soul to shreds,
It cuts like aching in her bones.
Remembering what was,
Her spirit yearns to touch what he and she will be

1. Isa 60:3–5; Rev 21:1–22:5

when two are reconnected in the Day.
She starts to pray:
How long, O LORD,
Before my heart no longer lingers in the cold
or stands apart?

What is your only hope in life and death?
Lift up your eyes and see the glory of the Lamb!
Look back and recognize His gifts of strength amidst your dark.
He carried you,
His arms have borne you in your darkest pain.
You stand because Compassion claimed a weary child
and took your hand.

What ugly subjugation
binds this dying world to sin!
How beautiful that He Who Conquers
chose to wear our onerous yoke,
Our slavery as His.
How unimaginable to us,
That He who knew no sin
would let its awful weight descend on Him.
The Lamb has carved our own eternal comforting
from sacrifice.
The Word sufficed to reconcile
the Wounded with the lost,
And He who bore the cost,
Who tabernacles,
Tents forever,

Leading us to join His holy place
where we will share
forever
In His fellowship and grace.

What is your only hope in life and death?
Lift up your eyes and see the glory of the Lamb!
Look now each time the bread and cup are passed,
Remembering what He has done on your behalf.
Let sacred glory linger here,
And let it touch your waiting while all worldly sorrows last.

Behold!
The dwelling place of God will be with man!
And this bright sanctuary
has no need of sun or moon,
For God's own glory gives it light.
His great salvation
has redeemed the unredeemable,
The undeserving
from their gross offense.
No more the dreadful fight to battle on.
No more accursed.
Kings and peoples,
Sons and daughters
gathering from every tribe and nation
come to worship Him,
To see Him face to face.

Death is dead!

No need to mourn.

The end of pain!

No weeping anymore.

The universe at last at peace.

For all the former things,

The shame,

The lies,

The growling, deep betrayal,

All the violence and hate

have ceased!

What is your only hope in life and death?

Lift up your eyes and see the Lamb!

Look forward to that glorious Day

when everything that crushed our souls

is blown away.

The hand that touched the unclean man

and healed his wounds,

That understands this sinner's fears,

This hand,

Will someday

reach to touch a tired face,

A human face,

And wipe away the remnants of remembered tears.

Look Up[1]

Look at the birds,
Our Savior says.
They neither sow nor reap,
Nor gather into barns,
And yet your heavenly Father feeds them.
Meeting all their needs,
He keeps their lives from harm.
Are you not more valuable than these?
We cannot disagree,
But here we hesitate.

We are like Peter,
Noticing the sea,
The waves.
There are so many waves.
Our fear would swallow up our feet
and drown our faith,
Forgetting it was Christ
who beckoned us to Him,
His glorious power reaching out to lift us over breaking swells.
Remembering,
That He,
Commanding storms to cease

1. Deut 7:6; Matt 6:26, 31–32

with just a word,

Can surely carry us through every day.

Look up,

We think,

Reminded of a thousand different ways His arm has borne us

through the raging surf

and we endured.

Look up,

We say,

And turn our eager faces toward His gaze,

Look up and join Creation's praise!

Morning Musings[1]

Old sun,
Slung low,
Its orange gaze
a tired eye
that overlooks a greying sky.
It is a sad and sober star
that stares upon this grubby dawn.

Hard to believe
this is my morning walk.
It feels more like fatigue
and age have drained the air.
So many wearied,
Worn,
Have crossed my path.
Too many struggle with despair.
A world of shadows beckoning
could swallow up a generation with its dread.
Perhaps,
I think,
It is an end to what I know.

1. Matt 27:51–53

But in the darkest moment
Man has ever seen,
The earth was shaken,
Rocks were split,
The curtain of the Temple ripped in two
from top to bottom,
Suddenly revealing
God's most Holy Place.
The tombs released the bodies of the saints,
Who wore their resurrection bodies into town
and went to check on neighbors
still above the ground.

Hard to believe
what possibly could happen here
in this stale,
Ancient world,
Or that eternal forces could unwrap
our time and space,
Except I know,
The universe that lifted up and raised the Son
has one more glorious Day to come.

The Age of Eternity[1]

I feel as if the world is falling down a rabbit hole,
And I am Alice,
Tumbling right behind.

I AM coming soon,
He says.

I understand this world is not a gentle place.
For sin has roughed the edges raw,
Has sanded down the quiet hills,
Has bent the trees,
Unearthed the mountains
underneath the tugging,
Wrestling pressures of the Curse,
And left us jagged boundaries,
Sharp and restless borders,
Pushing,
Pulling,
Cataclysmic wills demanding,
Redefining what was right,
Becoming What is Mine,
Until all human thoughts and deeds

---

1. Ps 88; Rev 22:6–21

express an awkward shape,
A monstrous wonderland design.

I AM the Alpha and Omega,
First and last,
Beginning and the end.
David's son and David's Lord,
I bring God's glory and His grace,
I wield the sword.

This wayward turning world seems vicious,
More intensely underlined,
More rough,
More angry,
Recently more violent.
I have felt the earnestness of darkness
spreading more and more,
Surrounding intellect and heart,
Its tangling,
Clinging arms confounding noble thought,
Its brash and bragging overriding simple truth
where even People of the Book
are falling through,
Are crumpling down,
Are floundering,
Hesitant and locked in fear.
I am afraid,
And I contend
(if only silent conversations in my head)

With this world's minor prophets,
Seers of the news and social media,
Panderers of broken wisdom
crying in the streets,
Demanding that we eat
their doomed philosophies as royal feasts.

Let evildoers still do evil,
And the righteous still do right.
I am coming soon,
And I will bring my recompense,
Repaying everyone for what they've done.
Blessed are those who washed their robes in Jesus' blood.
Come enter in.
Enjoy the Tree of Life.
Outside,
The lovers of the Liar
face a thousand times ten thousand daily deaths in fire.

The Spirit and the Bride say
Come!
Let the one who hears say
Come!
He who testifies says,
Surely, I AM coming soon!

Amen!
We say,
Come Lord Jesus! Come!